The Devil's Cloth

EUROPEAN PERSPECTIVES

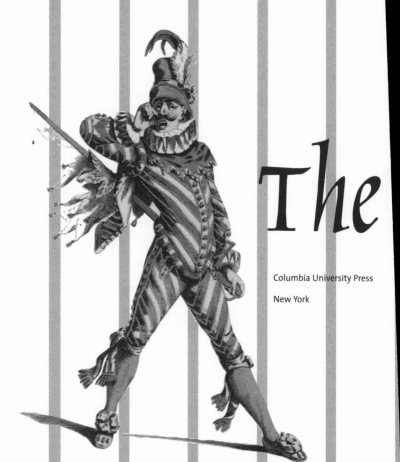

The

Columbia University Press

New York

Devil's Cloth

A HISTORY OF STRIPES AND STRIPED FABRIC

MICHEL PASTOUREAU   TRANSLATED BY JODY GLADDING

European Perspectives

A Series in Social Thought and Cultural Criticism

LAWRENCE D. KRITZMAN, EDITOR

European Perspectives presents outstanding books by leading European thinkers. With both classic and contemporary works, the series aims to shape the major intellectual controversies of our day and to facilitate the tasks of historical understanding.

For a complete list of books in the series, see pages 129–30.

for Anne

Columbia University Press wishes to express its appreciation for assistance given by the government of France through the Ministère de la Culture in preparation of this translation.

COLUMBIA UNIVERSITY PRESS

Publishers Since 1893

New York   Chichester, West Sussex

Copyright © 1991 Editions du Seuil. Collection La librairie du XXe siècle, sous la direction de Maurice Olender.

Translation and preface copyright © 2001 Columbia University Press

All rights reserved

Library of Congress Cataloging-in-Publication Data

Pastoureau, Michel, 1947–

   [Etoffe du Diable, English]

   The Devil's cloth : a history of stripes and striped fabric / Michel Pastoureau ; translated by Jody Gladding.

     p.   cm. — (European perspectives)

   Includes bibliographical references and index.

   ISBN 0–231–12366–3

     1. Costume—History 2. Costume in art—History 3. Stripes I. Title. II. Series.

   GT520 .P3713 2001

     391'.009—dc21

                                                            00–065831

Casebound editions of Columbia University Press books are printed on permanent and durable acid-free paper.

Printed in the United States of America

Designed by Linda Secondari

c 10 9 8 7 6 5 4 3 2 1

Contents

Illustrations

Preface to the American Edition

IN HIS AREAS OF EXPERTISE, the university historian publishes two relatively different kinds of books: books he does not initiate, commissioned by publishers or institutions, and books he himself plans and, once finished, must place with a publisher. Clearly, it is this second kind he holds most dear because there he can best present his research and his ideas. But these are the most difficult ones to publish, not only because the originality of bold, new work often prompts fear (at least in the social sciences) in editors charged with making decisions that are commercial rather than intellectual but also and especially because the author does not want to botch the execution of a book he has conceived and carried like a child, and to which he wants, justifiably, to give the best of himself. In doing this, without a deadline, not subject to the constraints of any series, completely free to say what he has wanted to say, the author takes his time, carefully conducts his inquiries, refines his ideas, perfects his style. In some cases, this leads him far from the initial project; in others, that project fails. Often, indeed, the author must give priority to commissioned work—especially collective works—and forever put off "for later" the writing of the book or books to which he attaches the most importance. Thus, among the books a researcher produces, these are not the most numerous.

Despite its brevity, *The Devil's Cloth* belongs to that category of works long considered, continually tinkered with, put aside for collective or commissioned work. However, the idea of abandoning it never crossed my mind, and even if much time has passed between its conception and its completion, I have been very happy to see it through. Among the thirty-five or so books I have now published, it is the only one that, once finished, truly corresponds to what I had hoped to write at the outset. Thus, great was my joy in seeing it take its place in Maurice Olender's prestigious series, La librairie du XXe siècle, published by Seuil, and just as great was my pride in subsequently seeing it translated into about fifteen languages, among them now English for the present American edition.

The idea for such a book came to me from daily contact with medieval documents. As a young researcher, I had observed that in images and in a certain number of texts, the figures wearing striped clothes were, in one way or another, negative figures. From then on, I sought to learn more, to understand the origin and the reasons for such a sign, to study its purposes and its variations, and then to inquire beyond the Middle Ages to learn how this sign developed, evolved, or was transformed in the modern and contemporary era. In short, I wanted to write a history of stripes and striped fabric in Western societies from the central Middle Ages until today. To do that, cloth and clothing were my two main themes.

Indeed, in most societies, the world of fabric is where questions of technique and material mingle most closely with questions of ideology and symbol. For the historian and the anthropologist, cloth and clothing always constitute places for multidisciplinary research. That is particularly true for medieval Christian societies in the West. The only real "industry" they knew was weaving cloth, and they articulated most of their social taxonomies around the signs and practices of dress.

In medieval dress, everything means something: the fabrics (material, texture, source, decoration), the pieces and forms, the colors (quality of the dyes, solidity, luminosity, tones, and shades), the work of cutting and assembling, the dimensions, the accessories, and, of course, how the clothes are worn. It is a matter of using conventional and always carefully coded signs to express a certain number of values and to ensure the corresponding verification of them. Everyone must wear the clothes of his state and rank. To dress more lavishly or more shabbily than is customary for the class or the circle to which one belongs is a sin of pride or a mark of debasement. Moreover, it is a transgression against the social order and thus a cause for scandal, like the one provoked in the thirteenth century by the Carmelites' striped cloak. Throughout, the classifying function of clothing overshadows its utilitarian function. Well before serving as protection against the effects of weather (people dress nearly the same way all year round and from one end of Western Christendom to the other) or being adapted to this or that physical activity, clothing tells who someone is by stressing membership in a group (familial, political, domestic, professional, military, religious, ethnic, or cultural). The stripe is one of the signs used to do this. Medieval dress thus appears as an institutional and prescriptive constraint and not as an individual practice, whether emotional, aesthetic, playful, or psychological. One doesn't wear the clothes one likes but the clothes that must be worn (and are things so different today?).

It is a shame that for such a long time historians, both medievalists and modernists, have not been interested in clothing and dress practices. They have relegated these domains to "historical footnotes" and to the works of amateurs, or have even contented themselves with one archeological study on the forms of dress, a study considered successively from the romantic, the aesthetic, and the positivist perspectives. Now this is clearly not what the phenomenon of dress involves. There is nothing anecdotal or romantic, not to mention aesthetic, about clothing; it is a veritable social system. Fortunately, in the past generation or two, under the influence of anthropology, sociology, and semiology (let us think here of Roland Barthes's pioneering work, *Le système de la mode* [The Fashion System], first published in 1967), a few historians have undertaken new inquiries, considering dress as a historical subject entirely by itself and dress practices as fully transdisciplinary and transdocumentary terrain. But in my opinion, there is still an immense gap between the richness of the subject and the all too rare studies we have at our disposal.

What is true for clothing in actual society is even more true in iconographic society. Here more than anywhere else, dress is a medium for signs and a tool for classification. Indeed, in images, attributes and codes are always more pronounced, more systematic, and more diffuse than in reality. More than ever it is necessary to know what we are dealing with. But here two axes intersect—a social axis and a moral axis—requiring the image to prove how supple and subtle it can be with regard to its codes and its behavior. Not only must figures of noble birth be distinguished from those situated lower on the social ladder, but those looked upon favorably from a moral standpoint must be highlighted, as well as those who, for one reason or another, have earned or are causing disgrace. There are the nobility and the peasants, and there are the good and the bad. Now these two axes do not necessarily overlap—far from it: there exist bad kings or bad princes, just as there exist virtuous artisans and model servants; there exist cruel and bloodthirsty pagan emperors and destitute but generous Christian serfs; there exist treacherous knights and commoners full of courage and nobility. The image must say all that and say it with subtlety, as it also must emphasize a figure's belonging to this or that group, the motivations driving him in this or that scene, and his relationships with other figures. To do this, clothing—with its forms, colors, decoration, insignias, and accessories—is always a privileged attribute. It follows codes, some of which recur throughout different categories of images and documents (that is the case with stripes) and others of which are more specific to this or that document, this or that artwork, this or that artist or studio. In the image, clothing is always the bearer of important meanings.

That is why, here again, it is a shame there are so few works on this subject. A good number of art historians, for example, have no idea of the wealth of information they could draw from analyzing the clothing presented in a work of art or group of images. Others grant iconography only a secondary role and prefer, now and forever, to devote themselves to tasks considered more noble: the study of style (but what is style?) and artists' biographies (often transformed into hagiographies). They are undoubtedly wrong. For the medieval and modern periods, iconography is always the most fruitful branch of art history, because it is the one that fully succeeds in making this discipline—as difficult and often ill-treated, if not scorned, as it is—into an authentic historical science. May the present book and the example of striped clothing bear witness to that.

The Devil's Cloth

Veste, quae ex duobus
texta est, non indueris
—Leviticus 19.19

Order and Disorder of the Stripe

"CET ÉTÉ, OSEZ LE CHIC DES RAYURES" [This summer, dare to be stylish in stripes]. In this somewhat flashy slogan displayed widely on the walls of the Paris metro in an advertising campaign several months ago, all the words are important. But the one which, it seems to me, carries the most weight is the verb, *oser*, dare. To wear stripes, to present oneself dressed in striped clothing—if we believe the slogan—is neither neutral nor natural. To do so, you must display a certain audacity, overcome different ideas of propriety, not be afraid to show off. But the one who dares is rewarded: he attains *chic*, style, that is, the elegant distinction of individuals who are free, at ease, refined. As is so often the case in our times, when any social code is capable of reversing itself, when any code, to function properly, is even required to reverse itself, what originally constituted a handicap or a liability ends up becoming an asset.

For the historian, this is food for thought. There's a great temptation to pass over the centuries and establish a link between the supposed boldness of contemporary stripes and the frequent scandals they prompted throughout the Middle Ages. In the long run, the stripe problem certainly exists, and clothes provide the most visible medium for it.

In the medieval Western world, there are a great number of individuals—real or imaginary—whom society, literature, and iconography endow with striped clothing. In one way or another, they are all outcasts or reprobates, from the Jew and the heretic to the clown and the juggler, and including not only the leper, the hangman, and the prostitute but also the disloyal knight of the Round Table, the madman of the Book of Psalms, and the character of Judas. They all disturb or pervert the established order; they all have more or less to do with the devil. Nonetheless, if it isn't very difficult to draw up a list of all those transgressors in striped clothing, it is harder to understand why such garments were chosen to designate their negative status. All the more so because there's nothing circumstantial or esoteric in this practice. On the contrary, beginning from the twelfth and thirteenth centuries, abundant documentation in all areas emphasizes the demeaning, pejorative, or clearly diabolic quality of striped dress.

Is this a cultural issue, the Christian Middle Ages having inherited earlier value systems and believing they found in the scriptures a justification for condemning striped clothes? Actually, among other moral or cultural prescriptions forbidding practices of mixing, the nineteenth chapter of Leviticus proclaims in verse 19: *Veste, quae ex duobus texta est, non indueris* [You will not wear upon yourself a garment that is made of two . . .]. Like the Septuagintal Greek translation, the Vulgate Latin text is not very explicit here. After *duobus*, we might expect a noun specifying the nature of what one is forbidden to combine with and on one's clothes. Are we to understand by this (as the word *texta* and many other passages in the Old Testament invite us to do): "You will not wear upon yourself a garment made of two different kinds textiles," that is, woven from wool (animal) and linen (vegetable)?[1] Or rather, are we to make the noun *coloribus* follow the adjective *duobus*, and understand it as "You will not wear upon yourself a garment made of two colors"? Modern translations of the Bible have retained the first solution, remaining faithful to the Hebrew text, but medieval exegetes and prelates have sometimes preferred the second and interpreted this as a ban on ornamentation and colors when it was only a question of fibers and cloth.

However, perhaps it isn't a matter (or only matter) of a scriptural problem, but of a visual problem? People in the Middle Ages seemed to feel an aversion for all surface structures which, because they did not clearly distinguish the figure from the background, troubled the spectator's view. The medieval eye was particularly attentive to reading by levels. Any image, any surface appeared to be built of layers, that is, cut out like raised pastry. An image was created by superimposing successive levels, and, to read it well, it was necessary—contrary to our modern habits—to begin with the bottom level and, passing through all the intermediary layers, end with the top one. Now, with stripes, such a reading is no longer possible. There is not a level below and a level above, a background color and a figure color. One and only one bichrome level exists, divided into an even number of stripes of alternating colors. With the stripe—as with the check, another pattern the medieval sensibility finds suspect—the structure *is* the figure. Is that where the scandal originates?

This book hopes to answer these various questions. But, in attempting to do so, it will not confine itself to the medieval period or to clothing. On the contrary, extending the history of stripes and striped cloth up to the end of our twentieth century, it sets out to show how, without in any way renouncing earlier uses and codes, each period has produced new ones, thereby bringing about an ever wider diversification in the stripe's physical and symbolic universe. Thus the Renaissance and the romantic periods expanded the uses of "good" stripes (signs of celebrations, exoticism, or freedom) without eliminating the bad ones at all. And the contemporary period has very much made itself the receptacle of all these practices and all the earlier codes, since coexisting within it are stripes that remain diabolic (those by which prisoners in the death camps were ignominiously marked) or dangerous (those used for traffic signs and signals, for example), and others that, over time, have become hygienic (those on sheets and underwear), playful (those used for children's things), athletic (those used for leisure and sports clothes), or emblematic (those on uniforms, insignia, and flags).

The medieval stripe was the cause of disorder and transgression. The modern and contemporary stripe has progressively transformed into a tool for setting things in order. But if it organizes the world and society, the stripe itself seems to remain unwilling to serve any organization too rigorous or too limited. Not only can it function through any medium, but it can be its own medium and, in doing so, open out into the exponential and the imperceptible. All striped surfaces can thus constitute one of the lines in another, larger, striped surface, and so on. The semiology of the stripe is infinite.[2]

That's why it is more to the social history than to the semiological stakes that the following chapters are devoted. The problem of the stripe does indeed lead to pondering the relationship between the visual and the social within a given society. Why, in the West, over the very long term, have the majority of social taxonomies expressed themselves most importantly through visual codes? Does the eye classify things better than the ear or the sense of touch? Is to see always to classify? That isn't the case either in every culture or in the animal world. Even so, why is the derogatory sign system, the one that draws attention to outcast individuals, dangerous places, or negative virtues, more heavily stressed (and thus more visible) than the status-enhancing sign system? Why is the historian more comfortable in the documentary terrain of the pejorative than of the laudatory?

Difficult and complex questions that can only be given brief answers. First, because this book intends to remain brief.[3] Second, because the stripe is such a dynamic surface structure that it can only be covered at a run. The stripe doesn't wait, doesn't stand still. It is in perpetual motion (that's why it has always fascinated artists: painters, photographers, filmmakers), animates all it touches, endlessly forges ahead, as though driven by the wind. In the Middle Ages, Fortune, who turns the wheel of destiny for man, often wears a striped robe. Today, on a playground, the schoolchildren in striped clothes always seem more active than the others. And in the area of sports, striped shoes run faster than single-colored ones.[4] Thus a book devoted to stripes must show itself capable of haste and swiftness.

The Devil and His Striped Clothes
(13TH–16TH CENTURIES)

EVERY SCANDAL LEAVES behind it evidence and documents. By the same token, the ancient historian has a better grasp on transgressions of the social order than on the social order itself. That is the case at the end of the Middle Ages with regard to stripes and striped clothing. There's hardly any documentation for plain fabric because it represents the ordinary, the quotidian, the "norm." For the stripe, on the other hand, there's plenty, because it causes disorder, because it makes some noise.

The Carmel Scandal

Scandal broke out in France in the middle of the thirteenth century. At the end of the summer of 1254, to be precise, when Saint Louis returned to Paris after an unsuccessful crusade, a dramatic captivity, and a stay in the Holy Land of four long years. The king did not return alone. He brought with him a number of monks newly arrived in France and, among them, a few brothers of the Carmelite Order. It was because of them that the scandal would ensue: they wore striped cloaks!

The Carmelites originated in the twelfth century when a few hermits established themselves near Mount Carmel in Palestine in an attempt to rediscover the life of prayers and mortification that the first Fathers had lived in the desert. According to the tradition, a Calabrian knight, Berthold, assembled them in 1154. Afterward, pilgrims and crusaders came to swell the ranks of the original group. In 1209, the patriarch of Jerusalem provided them with a set of rules based on extreme asceticism. This was, however, eased a little later by Pope Gregory IX who permitted them, most notably, to live in town and to devote themselves to preaching. Thus the Carmelites were classified with the mendicant orders, like the Franciscans and the Dominicans. What's more, their structures were modeled on the latter's, and like all the mendicant orders, the Carmelites began to teach in the universities, in Bologna and Paris.[5] There were difficulties in the Latin realm of Jerusalem, continually menaced by Muslim pressures, which forced them to leave the Holy Land for good. In fact, they had expanded into the West a few years before Saint Louis's return (for example, they were in Cambridge beginning from 1247), but, regarding the affair that interests us, it was very much their arrival in Paris in 1254 that marked the debut of a polemic on clothing spanning many decades.

We possess no contemporary iconographic evidence on mid-thirteenth century Carmelite dress. Textual evidence, on the other hand, abounds. There is hardly any agreement on the color of the robe—brown, fawn, gray, black, always dark in any case—but there is agreement on the cloak's design: it is striped, either white and brown or, more rarely, white and black. A legend explaining the biblical and celestial origin of this cloak appears early on. It was supposed to be a copy of the cloak worn by the prophet Elijah, Carmel's mythic founder. Carried off to the sky by a chariot of fire, he supposedly threw his great white cloak to his disciple, Elisha, and it was said to have retained, in the form of brown stripes, the burned traces of his passage through the flames. A lovely legend of origins, bringing into play one of the biblical figures most fascinating to men of the Middle Ages. Elijah, a messianic hero, is one of the rare scriptural figures who doesn't die. It emphasizes, moreover, the symbolic value of the investiture by the cloak. For medieval culture, any cloak is a medium for signs, and any handing over of a cloak is linked to a rite of passage, to entering into a new state.

Certain texts from the end of the thirteenth century push the symbolic gloss further, specifying that the Carmelite cloak was striped with four white bands representing the four cardinal virtues (strength, justice, prudence, and temperance), separated by three brown bands evoking the three theological virtues (faith, hope, love). In actuality, no rule ever codified either the number or the width or the direction of the stripes on the Carmelite cloak. And, in later iconographic documents, all variations collide: narrow stripes, wide stripes, vertical stripes, horizontal stripes, diagonal stripes; they don't seem to have any particular importance or meaning. What matters is that the cloak is striped, that is, it isn't plain and it doesn't resemble those worn by other orders—mendicant, monastic, or military—in a word, it deviates. In fact, it deviates so greatly that, despite itself, it approaches transgression.

Immediately upon their arrival in Paris, the Carmelites are the victims of mockery and abuse from the populace. People point and shout insults at them; they are ridiculed with the nickname "*les frères barrés*" [the barred brothers], a particularly pejorative expression, as *barres* in old French designates not only stripes but also the various marks of illegitimacy (a meaning that is retained in heraldry).[6]

Paris has no monopoly on jeering. In the towns of England, Italy, Provence, and Languedoc, and in those of the Rhone and Rhine river valleys, the newly established Carmelites are victims of the populace in the same way. Sometimes actions are combined with words, and physical violence accompanies verbal abuse. The Carmelites are often "put down," as are the Dominicans and the Franciscans. But what those latter are criticized for, who, like the Carmelites, live in town among the laity (and not in isolated abbeys, like the monks) is not just the appearance of their clothing.[7] They are accused of greed, hypocrisy, and treachery, and they are seen as henchmen for the devil and the Antichrist. As for the poor Carmelites, who also live by begging but whose order is less powerful, less influential with the princes, less linked to the instruments of religious or political repression, they are criticized above all for wearing striped cloaks.

Nevertheless, in Paris itself, another grievance is added, that of being a little too friendly with the Beguines, their closest neighbors on the right bank of the Seine. In one of his violent diatribes against the mendicant orders, which he accuses of having become the evil masters of Paris, the poet Rutebeuf is scandalized by this proximity and its possible consequences:

Li Barré sont prés des Béguines,
Souvent en ont a lor voisines:
Ne lor faut que passer la porte ...[8]

[The Barred are near the Beguines,
Often have them as their neighbors:
They only have to go through the door ...]

But everywhere the big problem remains the barred, that is, the striped cloak. At the beginning of the 1260s, the scandal reached such proportions in urban areas that Pope Alexander IV expressly ordered the Carmelite monks to abandon their striped cloaks for plain ones. Refusal. Polemics. Threats. The conflict grew more bitter and prolonged. It would last more than a quarter of a century, pitting the Carmelites against ten successive popes. In 1274, at the universal council of Lyon, the Carmelites' intransigence on this matter almost cost them their very existence. If their order was not abolished like about twenty other "secondary" mendicant orders, it was only because their new general superior, Pierre de Millaud (1274–1294), promised to submit to pontifical will and settle this question of cloaks as quickly as possible. In fact, it took another thirteen years, thirteen long years of debates, negotiations, promises, retractions. Finally, in 1287, at the general chapter in Montpellier, on the day of the feast of Mary Magdalen, the brothers decided to renounce the "barred" cloak and to adopt in its place an all white cope. But some Carmelites in distant provinces, in the Rhineland, Spain, and Hungary, refused to comply and continued to wear that scandalous piece of clothing until the first years of the fourteenth century. Nevertheless, in 1295, in a specially declared bull to this effect, Pope Boniface VIII confirmed the 1287 change in cloaks and solemnly restated the absolute ban against wearing striped habits for monks of all religious orders.[9]

Striped Fabric, Bad Fabric

Why such a ban? Why this disdain for the stripe and such general disgrace for those who wear it? Some nineteenth-century scholars believed that what was reproachable about the Carmelite cloak was its being Oriental, a Muslim cloak, a sort of striped jellaba like you still see today in Islamic countries. The scandal would then derive from Christian monks wearing cloaks like those of the infidels. A few decades earlier, hadn't Frederick II also shocked all Christendom by living and dressing like a "Saracen" in his Palermo palace? What's more, since the eighteenth century, the Carmelites themselves have sometimes explained that their old "cloak of infamy" had been imposed on them in Syria by Muslim authorities, the Islam tradition forbidding Christians to wear white clothes because, according to the Koran, they are a sign of nobility and distinction.[10] This is a historicizing, almost positivist explanation, which may not be totally false but which hardly takes into account the scope of the problem, limiting it to the level of a simple ethnic or religious mark, whereas it's a matter of a much more profound cultural phenomenon.

Actually, the Carmelites' case is not an isolated one in the least. In the West, other groups and other individuals also suffer because of their striped clothes. Consequently, the origin and the reasons for the Carmelite cloak hardly matter. What does matter, which is fully documented history, is that the stripe is just as much of a deviation and causes just as much of a scandal when it appears on a juggler's robe, a prince's breeches, a courtesan's sleeves, even the walls of a church or an animal's coat as when it appears on a monk's cloak.

For the moment, let us stick to the domain of clothing. Since the end of the Carolingian period, there is abundant and varied evidence highlighting the discriminatory nature of stripes. On this subject, there is certainly no case as well documented as that of the Carmelites in the second half of the thirteenth century, but earlier (or later) texts are not rare, which, in the course of a sentence or a paragraph, make it clear how degrading it is in the medieval Western world to wear striped clothes.

First of all, there are the decrees, repeated over and over, of the diocesan synods, the provincial assemblies, and the universal councils, which forbid clerics to wear two-colored clothes, whether bicolor (*vestes partitae*), striped (*vestes virgatae*), or checked (*vestes scacatae*). Again in 1311, the council of Vienne, which legislated many issues involving clothing, repeated these bans with insistence.[11] But these continual reminders prove that they were not respected, despite the severe penalties to which offenders exposed themselves in many dioceses. Thus in Rouen, in 1310, a certain Colin d'Aurrichier, a cobbler and "said to be a cleric," was condemned to death because he was married and because he "had been caught in striped clothes."[12] In all ecclesiastical society, war is henceforth declared on stripes, especially those that alternate bright colors—red, green, or yellow—and thus create an impression of gaudiness, of *diversitas*. In the eyes of the legislating prelates, nothing could be more unseemly.[13]

Later, in lay society, there are customs, laws, and regulations that require certain categories of reprobates or outcasts to wear two-colored or striped clothes. In Germanic customary law of the early Middle Ages, and again in the famous Sachsenspiegal (a collection of Saxon laws compiled between 1220 and 1235), such attire is imposed on or reserved for bastards, serfs, and the condemned.[14] Likewise, in the sumptuary laws and the decrees concerning dress that proliferated in the towns of southern Europe at the end of the Middle Ages, it is sometimes the prostitutes, sometimes the jugglers and clowns, sometimes the hangmen who are required to wear either an entirely striped suit of clothing or, more often, an item of striped clothing: a scarf, dress, or aglet for prostitutes; breeches or hoods for hangmen; doublets or hats for the jugglers and clowns. Everywhere, it is a matter of imposing a visual sign indicating a deviation so that those who practice such trades not be confused with honest citizens. Elsewhere, notably in German towns, similar orders apply instead to lepers, cripples, "bohemians," heretics, and sometimes, but more rarely, Jews and all those who are not Christians.[15]

The function of these dress and sumptuary laws—which still await their historians[16]—is certainly ethical and economic, but it is also, and above all, ideological and social. It is a matter of instituting a kind of segregation based on dress, each person being required to wear the clothing that marks his or her sex, state, or rank. In such discriminatory systems, the stripe often appears as the mark par excellence, the one that shows up the best and that emphasizes most strongly the transgression (of one kind or another) against the social order. The stripe isn't a form, like the disc, star, or round piece of cloth (*la rouelle*) that Jews and Muslims sometimes had to wear. It's a structure. As is nearly always the case in medieval sensibility and symbolic systems, structure is given priority over form and color. The stripe, whatever its perimeter and colors, is more clearly pronounced—and thus more "effective"—than the color yellow, the pointed hat, or the *rouelle partie*.[17]

Finally, a third category of evidence is provided by literary texts which quite often ascribe striped emblems or clothing to characters presented as evil or negative. There are already examples of this in Latin literature from the Carolingian period, but in the twelfth and thirteenth centuries, it develops especially in vernacular texts, notably in chansons de geste and courtly romances. Treacherous knights, usurping seneschals, adulterous wives, rebel sons, disloyal brothers,

1. THE IGNOMINIOUS STRIPE:
three young women condemned to prostitution, saved
by Saint Nicholas
Painted mural, northern Italy, about 1340.

---

cruel dwarfs, greedy servants, they all may be endowed with stripes on heraldry or clothes. They bear them on their coats of arms, their banners, their horses' covers, or, more simply, their robes, surcoats, breeches, head gear.[18] These are the barred ones, and just the mention of these bars is enough to tell the reader who he is dealing with. Beginning from the mid-thirteenth century, the ignoble characters introduced in these texts appear in images, joining a whole procession of notorious traitors and reprobates that the iconography had already long represented in striped clothing.

Saint Joseph's Breeches

Indeed, from as early as before the year 1000, images in the Western world had acquired the habit of reserving a pejorative status for striped clothing. The first figures who are graced with them—at first, in illuminations, then in mural paintings, and later in other media—are biblical figures: Cain, Delilah, Saul, Salome, Judas. Like red hair, striped clothes constitute the usual attribute of the traitor in the Scriptures. Of course, just as they are not always redheads, Cain and Judas, for example, are not always in stripes; but they are so clothed more frequently than all other biblical figures, and those stripes, when present, are enough to reveal their treacherous characters.[19]

Beginning from the mid-thirteenth century, the list of "bad" characters dressed in such a way grows considerably, notably in the secular miniature. From then on, added to the biblical traitors are those of the narrative and literary texts mentioned in the paragraph above—the most famous example being Ganelon, the traitor in the *Song of Roland*—as well as a large troupe of outcasts and reprobates from all walks of life. These come, for the most part, from the social categories I spoke of regarding the dress rules of the late Middle Ages, the iconography and urban society relying henceforth on a shared code of representation. In the image as in the street, all those outside the social order are often marked in this way by a striped attribute or piece of clothing, whether because of a condemnation (forgers, counterfeiters, traitors, criminals) or because of an infirmity (lepers, hypocrites, the simple-minded, the insane), whether because they are employed in an inferior occupation (valets, servants) or an ignominious trade (jugglers, prostitutes, hangmen, to which the image often adds three contemptible tradesmen: the blacksmiths, who are the sorcerers, the butchers, who are the bloodthirsty ones, and the millers, who are the stockpilers and the tight-fisted ones) or because they are not or are no longer Christians (Muslims, Jews, heretics). All these individuals transgress the social order, like the stripe transgresses the chromatic order and the order of dress.

Because the stripe never comes alone. In order for it to "function," in order for it to take on its entire meaning, it must be combined with or opposed to other surface structures, the plain and the patterned above all, but also the *parti*,[20] the checked, the spotted, and the diamond-patterned. In a picture, striped clothes always constitute a difference, a deviation that in itself gives emphasis to the one who is dressed in them. This emphasis is most often negative. Sometimes, however, the code is more subtle, less Manichaean, and, instead of expressing some clearly pejorative idea, the stripe connotes ambivalence, even ambiguity. A pertinent example is found in the iconography of Saint Joseph.

For a long time, Saint Joseph is a little-valued figure in the West, reduced to the role of a minor character or an intruder. In medieval religious theater, he is even openly ridiculed. Vices, unknown in the gospels and meant to cause laughter, are attributed to him: stupidity (he doesn't know how to count), clumsiness, avarice, drunkenness above all. Likewise, in processions, the role of Joseph is often taken by the village or parish idiot, and this is sometimes true right up to the eighteenth century.[21] There is no lack of images, whether they are paintings, sculptures, or engravings, which, until the end of the Middle Ages, frequently make him into a bald and shaky old man, never shown alone, never placed in the foreground (even in Nativity scenes), always standing back in relation to the Virgin and the Child, indeed even in relation to the three kings, Saint Anne, and Saint Elisabeth. In fact, we must wait for the Renaissance to witness a true promotion of Joseph, linked in part, moreover, to that of the Holy Family.[22] From an old simpleton, he is gradually transformed into a more dignified man, still in the prime of life, represented as nurturing father or artisan carpenter. But, for a long time still, he will remain ambiguous (to believe that Jesus was conceived naturally is heresy). In fact, it is beginning from the Counter-Reformation, thanks to the Jesuits and baroque art, that Saint Joseph will gain definitive prestige. But it will not be until 1870 that he will be proclaimed patron of the universal Church.

Regarding the problem of the stripe, the most interesting period in Joseph iconography comes in the fifteenth century and at the beginning of the sixteenth. From then on, Joseph is less discredited than during the early Middle Ages or the feudal period, but he is still not totally respected, much less venerated. From which derives, in the images, a certain number of behaviors and attributes meant to highlight this particular status. Among these, one of the most frequent consists of giving him striped breeches, an attribute of dress that appears in the Mosel and Rhine regions at the end of the fourteenth century and that gradually spreads into northern Germany, the Netherlands, the Rhine Valley, and Switzerland. Until the years 1510–20, examples of this are relatively abundant in stained-glass windows, illuminations, and panel paintings. After that, they become more rare, but a few isolated examples can still be found in seventeenth-century engravings.[23]

Striped breeches is a more discrete mark than striped clothes, properly speaking. To dress Joseph in an entirely striped robe, tunic, or cloak would have been clearly degrading. Giving him striped breeches simply represents a kind of accent meant to emphasize his specific character. Here, the stripe functions more as a sign of ambiguity than infamy. Joseph is neither Cain nor Judas. He is nothing of the traitor. He is only different, *divers* in the language of fifteenth-century French, less blessed than the Virgin, less ordinary than common mortals, elevated in certain respects, lowered in others, father without being father, necessary but disturbing, different, ambiguous, outside the norm, all things the stripe expresses fully in the fifteenth-century image. Indeed, it cannot only indicate transgression of the social or moral order, distinguish servants from masters, henchmen from victims, the insane from the sane, the damned from the elect, but, more subtly, it can also make felt certain, less clear-cut nuances and levels within value systems. By the same token, the stripe appears simultaneously as an iconographic code and as a mode of visual sensitivity. A dual feature worth pausing over.

Plain, Striped, Patterned, Spotted

The medieval eye is particularly attentive to the materiality and structure of surfaces. This structure serves especially to locate places and objects, distinguish zones and levels, establish rhythms and sequences, associate, oppose, distribute, classify, and organize into a hierarchy. Whether it is a matter of walls and floors, fabric and clothing, implements of daily life, leaves on trees, the coats of animals, or the human body itself, any surface, whether natural or manufactured, is always a medium for classifying signs. Texts and images give us countless examples. Studying them leads to grouping surface structures into three large categories of signs: the plain, the patterned, and the striped, with many variations capable of expressing these last two (checks, for example, are only a superlative form of stripes for the medieval sensibility). Let us look at these three structures for a moment and the way they find a place in images and on objects.

The truly plain is rare and all the more remarkable for that. First, on a good number of materials, medieval techniques hardly allow for obtaining perfectly plain, smooth, clean, monochromatic surfaces (this is the case with cloth, for example). Also, artists and artisans are hesitant to leave very large areas empty and often give in to the temptation of filling them or "dressing" them with webbing, hatching, mottling, thus playing with contrasts in texture, density, luminosity, or material. In painted images, entirely and uniformly plain surfaces are far from being the norm; rather, they constitute an exception and a response to specific intentions, linked to highlighting this or that element in the picture. Indeed, the plain surface, when it is used alone, is relatively neutral. But when it is opposed to the striped, the spotted, the compartmentalized, in fact, any woven or worked surface whatever, it always expresses some kind of emphasis, positive or negative.

The patterned, on the other hand, is always taken as something good. It is a plain surface, enhanced and increased in density. It consists of a monochromatic surface on which small figures are presented at regular intervals, either geometric or borrowed from the repertoire of heraldry: dots, discs, stars, rings, crescents, clover leaves, fleurs de lis. Most of the time, the figures so arranged are in a lighter color than that of the surface which serves as their background. The patterned surface almost always expresses something formal, majestic, indeed even sacred. Which explains its use on certain royal insignia, on coronation robes, on many liturgical objects, and in numerous images highlighting the divine. The Virgin especially maintains a privileged relationship with patterned decor. As for the coats of arms of French kings, *d'azur semé de fleurs de lis d'or* [azure patterned with golden fleurs de lis], which is found on their shield and their banner but also on many other media, it constitutes the most perfect example of the medieval pattern. It is a sign of power, a cosmic decoration, a Marian attribute, and a symbol of sovereignty and fecundity all at once.[24] Furthermore, iconographically, any pattern represents a static image, rooted in its medium, coming face to face with the viewer. It doesn't relate anything; it doesn't describe anything; it is simply there.

The spotted is an irregular pattern. Not only are the little figures arranged in a disorderly fashion, but they are themselves an irregular form: no longer stars, discs, crescents, but misshapen motifs or simple blotches. As such, they convey an idea of disorder, confusion, transgression. Visually the boundary distinguishing the patterned from the spotted is not always clear, but symbolically it is a matter of two worlds situated opposite each other. On one side, the sacred; on the other, the diabolic. On the bodies of humans and animals, the spotted indeed serves to convey the idea of furriness, impurity, or disease. That which is spotted often has something to do with the pustular, the scrofulous, the bubonic. In a society where skin diseases are simultaneously the most serious, the most common, and the most dreaded—let us think here of the fate reserved for "lepers"—the spotted represents degeneration, being banned from the social order, the antechamber of death and hell. In fact, in pictures, demons and satanic creatures are often spotted.[25]

These creatures can also be striped, which, in some way, is less serious but more ambiguous. Indeed, the stripe is the opposite of both the plain and the spotted, to which it is often opposed. But it is also something else, a rhythmic, dynamic, narrative surface that indicates action, the passage from one state to another. In thirteenth-century miniatures, Lucifer and the rebel angels often have bodies covered with horizontal stripes, a lively sign of their fall. These stripes are also an accent: the spectator's eye cannot *not* be drawn to a striped surface. In any image, the striped element is the one seen first. Fifteenth- and sixteenth-century Flemish painters sometimes use a process that consists of placing a figure in striped clothes either in a central spot or at a focal point for the painting or panel, thus catching the viewer's eye the moment it connects with the work. Sometimes this striped figure functions as a veritable trompe-l'oeil. Memling, Bosch, Bruegel, and a few others are particularly skillful at thus highlighting not one of the principal actors in the scene or the story but a third-rate walk-on whose sole function is to momentarily divert our gaze from a more essential area of the painting which requires that it reveal itself slowly. In his famous *The Way to Calvary* (1563), for example, a painting of huge dimensions including more than five hundred figures, Bruegel placed an anonymous and perfectly insignificant peasant almost in the center of the composition, walking hurriedly, wearing a hat and a robe with white and red diagonal stripes. Because these stripes create a pronounced visual discrepancy with regard to what surrounds them, it is first to that peasant that the viewer's eye is directed, and not to the forefront of the painting where John and holy women attempt to support the weeping Virgin, and still less to the background of the scene where Christ, fallen under the weight of his cross, is lost, as though forgotten in the midst of an indifferent crowd.[26]

We may wonder about this "visual priority" given to the stripe in relation to other surface structures. What is striped is seen before what is plain, before what is patterned, even before what is spotted. Is this a phenomenon of perception specific to Western man? Or might it be something common to all cultures, indeed all humans and even certain animals? With such a phenomenon, does a boundary exist between the biological and the cultural, and, if so, where is it located? I will try to answer these difficult questions at the end of this book.

What can already be emphasized here is the link between the stripe and the idea of diversity in the Middle Ages, or *varietas*, as medieval Latin calls it. Striped (*virgulatus*, *lineatus*, *fasciatus*, etc.) and varied (*varius*) are sometimes synonymous, and this synonymy instantly pulls the stripe over to the pejorative side. Indeed, for medieval culture, *varius* always expresses something impure, aggressive, immoral, or deceitful. Someone characterized as *varius* is either full of cunning or a liar, either cruel or sick, especially if it is a matter of mental illness or skin disease. What's more, the noun form of *varietas* itself serves to designate deception, wickedness, and leprosy all at once.[27] And, of course, as we have seen in the images, figures who are disloyal (Cain, Judas), cruel (the hangman), stricken with "madness" (the court jester, the insane of the Book of Psalms), or even the sick (lepers, supposed descendants of lepers) are frequently given striped clothes. There is a huge gap between our contemporary sensibility—which turns "variety" into a positive value instead, connoting youth, cheerfulness, tolerance, an inquisitive mind—and the sensibility of people of the Middle Ages, who invested above all in that notion of pejorative values. A good Christian, an honest man, cannot be *varius*. The *varietas* has to do with sin and hell.

That is equally true for animals. Those with coats either striped (*tigridus*) or spotted (*maculosus*) are creatures to fear. They can be cruel and bloodthirsty like the tiger, hyena, and leopard (the medieval leopard, which bears little relation to the true feline of that name, always symbolically represents a bad lion),[28] thieves like the trout or the magpie, sly like the snake or the wasp, diabolic like the cat or the dragon. Even the zebra, on whom Renaissance zoologists like to hold forth, passes for a dangerous animal at the end of the Middle Ages. Certainly these authors have never seen one and know little about them (they consider them a kind of donkey or onager); but because they know they are striped, they make them into cruel and diabolic creatures and include them in Satan's bestiary.[29] Later, we will see how this misunderstood animal will be promoted again in the Age of Enlightenment.

What's more, without calling on the exotic bestiary, all horses with coats not one uniform color are mounts that lower the status of those riding them. In literary texts, and notably in chivalric tales, one topos often opposes the hero, mounted on a white horse, and the traitor, the bastard, or the stranger, mounted on a horse of many colors: painted, dappled, piebald, bay, roan, etc.[30] Although occurring in a whole other context, a similar value system is found again in the *Roman de Renart*. The animals with striped coats (Grimbert the badger) or spotted ones (Tibert the cat) line up on the side of the animals with red coats (Renart the fox, Rousseau the squirrel) and constitute the clan of liars, thieves, lechers, and money grubbers. For animal society as for human, to be red-haired, striped, or spotted amounts to almost the same thing.

This mistrust, this fear, even, of spotted or striped animals has left an enduring mark on the Western imagination. As late as the eighteenth century, the famous beast of Gévaudan, which, in 1764–67, spread terror to the borders of Auvergne and Vivarais, is described by all who saw it, or thought they saw it, as a gigantic wolf with wide stripes on its back.[31] A diabolic creature, this "beast" of Gévaudan could not *not* be striped. Following it, each of the other "beasts of Gévaudan," which troubled the minds and the countryside of most of the French provinces for several decades, sometimes right up to the middle of the nineteenth century, was seen as striped as well.[32] Let us observe, moreover, that still today in our contemporary mythology, the tiger, which is only seen at the zoo and whose coat we admire, remains the very symbol of a fascinating kind of cruelty.

From a semiological point of view, that parallel which medieval culture draws between what is striped and what is spotted invites reflection on the very notion of surface structure. For us, a structure cannot begin without at least a ternary arrangement. For the medieval man, on the other hand, what is binary differs not in the least from what is ternary, quaternary, decanary, etc. On one side, there is the plain—and that same word, *plain*, is used in ancient French and the language of heraldry; on the other, there is everything that is not plain: the spotted, the striped, the divided, all structures that finally express the same values. This equivalence is found again in the domain of colors, where, likewise, the notions of bichromatic and polychromatic hardly differ. As for the prostitute, whose dress is striped red and yellow, and the juggler or the clown—future Harlequin—whose costume is made up of squares or diamonds of three, ten, twenty, a hundred different colors,[33] all three wear upon their clothing the very idea of trouble, disorder, noise, and impurity. Two colors are worth the same as ten colors; two stripes are worth the same as ten squares or a hundred diamonds. Striped, spotted, variegated, rainbow-colored may differ visually—especially in posing the problem of planes,[34] as we will see regarding coats of arms —but not conceptually or socially. They only convey varying degrees of the same state: that of transgression.

The Figure and the Background: Heraldry and the Stripe

There is a model code in which the historian and the semiologist can attempt to dissect into all their ramifications the close ties which, in matters involving stripes, unite the visual problems and the social stakes: the blazon. By this word, we refer to the entirety of the rules, terms, and figures which serve to represent coats of arms.

Appearing in the twelfth century for reasons both military (to identify combatants on the battlefields and in tournaments) and social (to give marks of identity to the upper classes in feudal society), coats of armor can be defined as colored emblems, belonging to an individual or a group of individuals, and subject to a few rules regarding their composition. Essentially it is these rules, not numerous but very prescriptive, that distinguish the European heraldic system from all other emblematic systems, before or after. Beginning from the middle of the twelfth century, the spread of coats of arms was extremely rapid, as much in geographic as in social space. By about 1300, all Western society could make use of them. Nothing prevented an individual from adopting the coat of armor of his choice, the only condition being that he not usurp someone else's. Thus the heraldic system was at its height. Signs of identity, marks of possession, and ornamental motifs all at the same time, coats of arms appeared on media of all kinds: civilian and military clothes, buildings and monuments, furniture and cloth, books, seals, currency, art objects, and objects from everyday life. The churches themselves gave much space to them and were often transformed into veritable heraldic museums.[35]

Countless coats of arms include "stripes" in one way or another. Perhaps 15 percent of the million medieval coats of arms in the current inventory for Western Europe. But various realities lie hidden behind this percentage. In heraldry, there are stripes, and then there are stripes. From the formal point of view, variants and subvariants can be multiplied to infinity. And, from the symbolic point of view, it makes quite a difference if those stripes appear in coats of arms belonging to actual individuals or families or if they appear in coats of arms attributed to literary or imaginary figures. Indeed, when they include "striped" figures, the first type are neutral, symbolically, while the second type are highly pejorative. Let us examine this in closer detail.

The vocabulary of the blazon doesn't contain the words *stripes* and *striped*. It doesn't even possess a generic term to designate the entire set of striped figures and structures. On the other hand, it carefully distinguishes those stripes that result from cutting up a plane into a certain number of lines or bands (these are partitions) and those that are simply set down on a single plane (these are pieces). In the first case, the number of bands is even, there is only one plane, and the two colors are perfectly balanced. In the second, the number of bands is uneven, there are two planes, and the dominant color is the background one. For the blazon—and for the medieval eye in general—true stripes are partitions, that is, those that make the figure and the background merge into a single plane. Visually, it is impossible to say which is the color of the figure and which is the color of the background. There is only one plane (whereas in the patterned or the spotted there are two, that of the background and that of the spots or pattern figures), and nevertheless the surface of this single plane is not plain! That in itself already constitutes something odd, something perverse, which opens the door to scandal. All striped surfaces seem to cheat, since they forbid the eye to distinguish the figure from the background on which it rests. Reading in layers, beginning from the background plane and advancing to the plane closest to the eye of the spectator, which is the usual procedure for reading images in the medieval period, becomes impossible. The "laminated" structure, to which the medieval gaze is so sensitive and so accustomed, has disappeared, and the eye no longer knows where to begin its reading or where to look for the background of the image. By the same token, all striped surfaces seem perverse, almost diabolic.

Extremely sophisticated, moreover, the blazon possesses a precise and multiple vocabulary for qualifying and differentiating the coats of arms formed by horizontal stripes (*fascé*), vertical stripes (*palé*), left to right diagonal stripes (*bandé*), and right to left diagonal stripes (*barré*). These are four different surface structures. The first three are frequently encountered. The fourth is rare (except in Italy) and, because it is rare, possesses a certain pejorative connotation. Like the barred cloak of the Carmelites, barred coats of arms have gotten bad press for a long time and, in heraldic literature, have sometimes been reserved for treacherous knights and figures of ignoble birth, especially bastards.

But the blazon goes further still. Beginning from these four basic striped structures, it constructs a throng of variants by playing simultaneously with the number and the thickness of the stripes, and especially with the form of the lines defining them: straight, curved, broken, wavy, etc. Let us take the example of a horizontally striped shield. It is called *fascé* if the number of stripes—always even—is higher than eight but becomes *burelé* beginning from ten. The *fascé* itself becomes *fascé-ployé* when its boundary lines are curved, *fascé-ondé* when they are wavy, *fascé-crénelé* when they are notched, *fascé-dentelé* when they are cut into little teeth, *fascé-vivré* when the teeth are more exaggerated. The system is infinite and the code always open-ended.

These geometric and lexicographic exercises surrounding the stripe are not mere speculation or gratuitous amusement. On the contrary, in relying on figures that are simple and easy to represent, they allow heraldry not only to provide the whole of society with coats of arms but also to establish groupings and articulate links of kinship through them. Within the same family, the oldest branch could, for example, carry a shield *fascé d'argent et d'azur* (that is, horizontally striped white and blue) and the younger branches carry shields with the same color stripes in the form of *fascé-ondé, fascé-vivré, fascé-crénelé*. Visually, the effect produced is sufficiently homogeneous to highlight the cohesion of the family (all the shields resemble one another), but at the same time it introduces differences (the blazon calls them *brisures*) helping to distinguish each branch. With a remarkable economy of means, coats of arms manage to express extremely subtle and complex kinship structures.

European heraldry is not the only one to resort to stripes and striped surfaces to convey kinship through images. In Asia, Africa, and especially South America, similar codes exist for the specific function of locating an individual within a group, and that group within the society. These codes nearly always appear on textile media, clothes, or clothing accessories. In Andean countries, for example, cloths with finely differentiated weaves or bands allow for distinguishing ethnicities, clans, or familial groups.[36] A similar system is found once more in Scotland by way of the tartans (whose history hardly dates back beyond the eighteenth century, even though the social structures on which they depend are different.[37] All the same, neither here nor elsewhere is the code so developed and refined as in the coats of arms themselves. What is more, as compared to the emblems used by other societies and cultures, coats of arms offer the particularity of being able to function on any kind of medium whatsoever: wood, stone, cloth, paper, metal, skin, etc. Formally, the same coat of arms can be drawn, painted, engraved, or modeled in a thousand different ways and remain the same coat of arms (in this sense, it can be compared to a letter in the alphabet). Also, in heraldry, structure always takes priority over form; the coat of arms is not an image but a structure of image. In the same way, any stripe, no matter what it is, is more or less essentially heraldic because it, too, is a structure before being a form.

Another original feature of the European heraldic system lies in the attribution of coats of arms to imaginary figures: literary heroes, biblical figures, mythological creatures, divine characters, personified vices and virtues. These attributions originate with the beginning of heraldry, that is, from the mid-twelfth century, and endure until the modern period. Thanks to these imaginary coats of arms, historians have at their disposal abundant material for studying the symbolic dimension of the blazon (which true coats of arms hardly allow for at all). By comparing what one knows and believes about a character and the heraldic figures or colors attributed to that character, it is possible to derive value systems and figure out what each of those figures or colors could have signified or connoted in the sensibility and imagination of the people of the Middle Ages.

As for stripes and striped figures, again we find in these literary and imaginary coats of arms all the pejorative aspects we have highlighted with regard to clothing and iconography. Most coats of arms bearing "stripes" are bad or negative coats of arms. Literary texts confer them on traitorous knights, usurping princes, figures of ignoble birth (bastards, commoners), and all those whose behavior is cruel, dishonest, or impious. In pictures, these imaginary coats of arms with stripes (*fascés*, *bandés*, *palés*, etc.) are generally given to pagan kings, diabolic creatures, and vices personified (especially infidelity, lying, and trickery). Of course, those heraldic figures constructed around the stripe don't represent the whole of bad figures—they share this role with many animals (leopard, monkey, goat, snake, dragon, toad) and with other geometric figures (the crescent and the checkerboard, for example)—but they constitute a good part of it.[38] Furthermore, thanks to the modifications in borderlines mentioned earlier, it is possible to create nuances and to distinguish levels within the pejorative: a knight provided with a *fascé* shield will thus be perceived as a treacherous knight, but one whose treachery is less serious than another knight given a *fascé-vivré* shield (horizontal stripes in the form of chevrons). Here again, there are stripes, and then there are stripes; they are all derogatory, but they are not so to the same degree or in the same fashion.

The question that presents itself to the historian is knowing how such a code is received and experienced. From the perspective of imaginary heraldry, all striped coats of arms, or nearly all, are negative. Whereas, in reality, a countless number bear stripes. Since at least the end of the twelfth century, the kingdom of Aragon, for example, bears on its coats of arms a *palé d'or et de gueules*, that is, vertical yellow and red stripes. These stripes, which may be Provençal in origin, are probably inherited from an ancient feudal banner, a visual sign to rally. They constitute an emblem of prestige and not a disparaging symbol.[39] How does the public manage with these discrepancies between true and imaginary coats of arms? How can such and such a family, such and such a prince, such and such a lord bear to have striped coats of arms when they know that, in many literary texts and works of art, similar coats of arms are attributed to bad characters? Is it a question of context? of reading level? of the receiver? In any case, the code of the blazon seems to be among the most highly effective here, since it is capable of grafting onto the same image structure two different (if not opposite) value systems.

A modern continuation of striped coats of arms can be read in flags. We will return to this later, but let us emphasize here that many European flags have in their distant origins some ancient feudal banner or even an ancient dynastic coat of arms. Now, any flag, whether for a nation or a state, is clearly not pejorative in the eyes of those using it. Here, the code has definitely broken off from its imaginary and negative aspect. A few traces, on the other hand, have survived in the system of livery and domestic clothing. Without being diabolic, the stripe has remained a depreciating mark.

From the Horizontal to the Vertical and Back
(16TH–19TH CENTURIES)

WITH THE MODERN PERIOD, a new order of the stripe gradually establishes itself. Without entirely losing any of its old characteristics, the
stripe takes on new forms and meanings. Henceforth its use in textiles
extends well beyond clothing and emblems: interior decor, furniture,
hygiene, daily life, and the nautical world make greater and greater use
of it. To this diversification in functions corresponds a diversification in
meanings. All stripes are no longer pejorative. On the contrary, the ancien régime sees the dawn of a "good" stripe, of a status-enhancing
stripe which, in the romantic period, not only announces "the dawn of
a new era" but even seems on the verge of overtaking the pejorative
stripe. At the same time, the predominance of horizontal stripes
abates and then disappears. Vertical stripes, which the Middle Ages
had only used sparingly, multiply. They favor the appearance of revised
structures and rhythms: strict adherence to two colors no longer de-
fines the stripe's terrain. The stripe can now be tricolor, quadricolor,

even polychromatic, and equidistance between the lines defining the stripes is no longer an absolute rule.

On clothing, this geometric variety allows the old social classifications to be overtaken. As the stripe is no longer diabolic—or rather, no longer only diabolic—a much larger share of society now wears it. In eighteenth-century Europe, we thus find, side by side, an aristocratic and a peasant stripe, a holiday stripe and an everyday stripe, an exotic stripe and a domestic stripe.

From the Diabolic to the Domestic

What characterizes the status of striped clothing at the end of the Middle Ages and the beginning of the modern age is a very rapid transition from the diabolic to the domestic. Whether independently or in association with their old connotations of impurity or transgression, stripes gradually become the primary sign of a servile condition or subordinate function. By the same token, their use is going to grow.

Actually, the appearance of these domestic stripes goes back to early times. If we search far, we will find examples of it in Rome during the imperial epoch.[40] Nevertheless, those that concern us here are different in essence and find their origin in the feudal period. They appear during the course of the eleventh century, a time when Western society provides itself with more and more taxonomic marks and when clothes become the privileged medium for registering most of these marks. Forms, colors, textures, motifs, decors, and accessories henceforth serve to classify individuals and groups, and, sometimes, to express the links of kinship, dependence, or relationship that unite them. Heraldry, as such, is still only in gestation, but this system of dress already fulfills a highly emblematic function, and it already makes wide use of stripes.

The first striped clothes of this kind, emphasizing an inferior condition but not necessarily pejorative or diabolic (even though, in the feudal period, it is difficult to completely separate these different notions), seem to have been worn by the domestic staffs of lords: first, palatine serfs, kitchen and stable boys, table waiters; later, men of arms and the hunt, grooms, sergeants, provosts, ministers of all kinds. After that, during the course of the twelfth century, this use of stripes on clothes extends to all those who fulfill some charge or who live off lordly generosity: cup bearers, chambermaids, hunters, falconers, heralds, clowns, musicians. The list varies according to region and decade. According to the documentation, as well, images giving a more numerous and diversified picture than the texts. It certainly seems as though it was in the Germanic countries, and especially in the Rhine area and in southern Germany, that this practice developed earliest. It is also there that it would continue throughout the entire Middle Ages and last well into the modern period.[41]

After the appearance of coats of arms, about the middle of the twelfth century, these domestic dress stripes and the code of the blazon link up in a certain way. The bicolor stripes of domestic personnel and officers in the service of a lord henceforth take on the heraldic colors of that lord, even if the lord himself has no stripes in his coat of arms. This is where we must locate the birth of what will later be called livery. Furthermore, little by little, a sort of equivalence will be established between heraldic *mi-parti* dress—that is, divided vertically in two halves of different colors—and striped clothing. This equivalence will last until the end of the Middle Ages and will apply as much to domestic livery as to the dress worn by outcasts and reprobates of whom we have spoken earlier.[42] From the structural point of view, it is a good

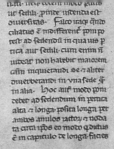

2. THE DOMESTIC STRIPE:
falconry servant taking care of a falcon
Miniature from a treatise on falconry by Emperor Frederick II, about 1240–50.

example in that it emphasizes the medieval equivalence (which would no longer be true today) between the simple bichromatic (*mi-parti*) and the bichromatic repeated in alternating sequences (stripes).

It also has a strong metonymical quality, since one piece or one area of clothing alone can be striped or bicolor and nonetheless apply to the entire outfit. This is frequently the case with breeches and sleeves (remember Saint Joseph) whereby bicolor sleeves are enough to convey a negative trait, whether moral or social. In medieval culture, the part always equals the whole.

Between the beginning of the fifteenth century and the middle of the sixteenth, the trend in domestic stripes reaches its height. It applies as much to men as to women. In images, servants in striped blouses, dresses, or aprons abound. Equally abundant, especially at the turn of the fifteenth to the sixteenth century, are pages, valets, and black slaves painted in striped clothing. The domestic stripe is coupled here with an important exotic dimension. This phenomenon is primarily Italian, especially Venetian, the high patricians of Venice sending for young adolescents from Africa destined to serve in their palaces.[43] This African touch rapidly becomes a style, extending to a large portion of the peninsula, and then beyond the Alps. Each palace, each court had its black "slaves," whom one took pleasure in dressing in stripes. These stripes expressed simultaneously Oriental origin (for medieval civilization, Africa is in the East), pagan birth, and servile condition. Even though in decline after 1560–80, this custom reappeared sporadically from the seventeenth to the nineteenth century.

This link that domestic service had established between the stripe and the black man left a deep mark in paintings and in engravings. As early as the end of the fifteenth century, for example, in many representations of the *Adoration of the Magi*, the black king was given striped clothing.[44] In the following century, that became a veritable iconographic attribute. All the same, Balthazar was not a slave in the least nor a lowly social figure; much the opposite. But the custom was gradually established of associating striped clothes and Africans, no matter what their social rank. Thus a painter like Veronese never misses an opportunity to dress the black men he portrays in stripes, or even—the refinement of a great artist imitating himself—to place beside every black man a white man in striped clothing.

This association between the black man and the stripe lasted a particularly long time in engravings, theater, and all entertainment or rituals in which disguise plays a part. To give oneself stripes throughout the modern period is enough to transform oneself into a "savage," to transgress the social and cultural order. Extending even beyond the framework of Africa, striped dress became the generic sign for all forms of exoticism or for life in the natural state.[45] American Indians, and later Oceania Indians, were also represented in stripes, either on their clothing or on their painted bodies. For the West, the stripe, or at least a certain stripe, had become the obligatory mark of the peoples considered most removed from "civilization."

For all that, domestic stripes didn't disappear. Heraldic or not, they traversed the entire ancient régime in the medium of livery and survived even until the middle of our century through means of the striped vest. Born in Victorian England, this article of clothing, often yellow and black, rapidly became the specific attribute of valets and butlers in Europe and the United States.[46] Today, its use is a bit outdated, but reminders of it remain very present in films, cartoons, and comic strips, three creative fields in which attributes of dress play an essential role, and where, thanks to the vertically striped vest, a butler cannot be recognized as anything but a butler. One of the most well-known is Nestor, Captain Haddock's butler, presented by Hergé in the adventures of Tintin. Whatever the circumstances, Nestor is perpetually dressed in his striped vest.

In England, at the end of the last century, domestics wearing such vests had acquired the nickname "tigers"; they were often Africans.

Domestic stripes, exotic stripes, and animal stripes (those of cats) merged into a single metaphor, more or less depreciating. For a long time, these "tigers" were no longer encountered in homes, but they were still present in advertising notices until the middle of the twentieth century.

Another continuation of the medieval stripe and the livery of the ancien régime is found in uniforms. First, civil uniforms (gamekeepers, town officers, subordinate civil servants of all sorts) and then military uniforms. Here again, stripes and heraldry joined to create systems of emblems, to organize groups, to establish a hierarchy for the positions of individuals within these groups. Within the military, these are the *lansquenets* (a French translation of the term *Landsknechte*—literally: "servants of the country"), German mercenaries serving the great powers, the very first of whom were distinguished by their striped clothing as early as the fifteenth century. Beginning from the seventeenth century, when the true uniform (in the modern sense of the word) was born, the military stripe, in combination with all sorts of ensigns, standards, and flags, extends to numerous corps of troops in most European countries. Later we will see how, by another approach, it touched the world of sailors as well.

From the Domestic to the Romantic

Parallel to the domestic stripe, which traverses the whole ancien régime uninterrupted, the modern period witnesses the diffusion of another category of stripes, no longer diabolic or derogatory, but, on the contrary, value-enhancing. This is an aristocratic stripe, sometimes sophisticated, always in good taste, fashionable in certain decades as early as the sixteenth century, and then triumphant in the second half of the eighteenth century in the first period of romanticism. It finds expression first on clothing, and then gradually on other textile media, especially upholstery material.

Actually, the phenomenon is already in gestation in many northern Italian towns as early as the end of the Middle Ages. In Venice, Milan, Genoa, about the middle of the fourteenth century, following the Great Plague, the joy of coming back to life again after such difficult trials led young nobles and rich patricians to all kinds of excesses in dress. Ranking first among these excesses, the wearing of partially striped clothes. These stripes especially appear on sleeves and breeches, and—a new tendency—they are not horizontal, as those then imposed on outcasts and reprobates, but vertical. Such an inversion somewhat mitigates the scandal that wearing striped clothes still and perpetually constitutes, but it isn't enough to overcome it completely. The idea of a transgression of the social and moral order—a transgression no doubt desired by those who presented themselves in this way—remains strong.[47] Faced with the laws and the authorities, this new fashion could last only a short time. After 1380 it became more discrete, without, however, disappearing altogether.

It remains in the shadows throughout the entire next century, while the strict Burgundian court imposes its values, its codes, and its leadership in protocol and dress on all of Europe. We have to wait for the end of the century and especially the turn of the fourteenth to the fifteenth century for the fashion in vertical stripes to experience a new boom, first in Germany, then in Italy, and later in France and England. Times changed, and these "modern" stripes no longer really suffered from the disgrace heaped on those that had preceded them. A few sovereigns even set the example and had their portraits painted in striped

3. THE STYLISH STRIPE:
mi-parti clothing worn by the courtly poet Rubin
von Rüdeger, taking his lady out to exchange
pleasantries in the forest
Miniature drawn from Codex Manesse, *northern Switzerland,
early fourteenth century.*

breeches or doublets (such as François I by Clouet, and Henry VIII by Holbein). The princes imitated them. The vertical stripe becomes aristocratic while the horizontal stripe remains, for the most part, servile. Only the Spanish court, heir to Burgundian austerity, resists this general movement, which seems to peak for the first time about 1520. After that, the Protestant Reformation, wars, economic difficulties, political and religious disturbances, and the Catholic Counter-Reformation all favor a return to more plain and somber clothing, which provides little opportunity for striped extravagances.[48]

Stripes experience a resurgence in the first half of the seventeenth century, by about the 1620s and 1630s. For two decades, Spanish fashion, then dominant, leaves a playful little opening in clothing where stripes try to intrude, especially in men's clothing (sleeves, bodices, breeches). In general, these are dark stripes, "caravagesque" stripes, that alternate ochres and browns, blacks and purples, sometimes greens and golds. This fashion involves only the aristocracy and doesn't last long. It ends at the same time as the Thirty Years' War, a little before the middle of the century. The *lansquenets* with their striped uniforms may have helped launch it, and no doubt also contributed to its demise.[49]

Then comes a long period without stripes, with a slight exception for court dresses and women's clothing accessories at the end of the century. But neither classical French taste nor Germanic or Italian baroque cultivates striped surfaces or clothing. Only a certain attraction for the East and things Turkish occasionally brings to the forefront a few exotic stripes. These become more numerous in France under the Regency, and then almost throughout Europe about the middle of the eighteenth century. People enjoy disguising themselves or pretending to be sultans or sultanas then, and very often a striped cloth is enough to add an Oriental touch to a costume.

Everything changes after 1775. In one decade, the decade of the American Revolution, the stripe, still rare and exotic a generation earlier, begins to invade the world of clothing, textiles, emblems, and decor. This is the beginning of the romantic and revolutionary stripe, born in the New World, but which is going to find the soil of old Europe particularly fertile ground. In fact, it is the beginning of a very widespread phenomenon that will last more than half a century, involving all social classes and profoundly transforming the visual and cultural status of stripes and striped surfaces.

The explosion of this new order of the stripe was favored by the decline of the pejorative character it had had since the Middle Ages. Without disappearing completely—later, we will see how it is still present in our contemporary societies—this pejorative aspect, still very marked in the seventeenth century, becomes more discrete and more circumstantial in the following century. Typical in this regard are the treatises by naturalists on the zebra and the place accorded this animal in the value systems. While zoologists in the sixteenth century and at the beginning of the seventeenth century considered this "wild donkey" to be a dangerous and imperfect, even impure, animal, Buffon, on the contrary, saw it to be one of the most harmonious of creatures: "Perhaps of all four-legged animals, the zebra is the most well made and the most elegantly dressed; it has the figure and grace of the horse, the lightness of the deer, and its coat, striped with black and white bands, arranged with so much regularity and symmetry, makes it seem as though nature used a ruler and compass to paint it. The alternating bands of black and white are all the more remarkable because they are narrow, parallel, and precisely divided, as in striped cloth; they extend not only over the whole body but over the head, the thighs, the legs, and all the way to the ears and tail. In the female, these bands alternate black and white; in the male, they are black and yellow, but they are always a lively and brilliant shade on the short, fine, thick coat, its luster augmenting the beauty of the colors."[50]

Buffon is the son of the Enlightenment; stripes do not disturb or disgust him, as was the case for his predecessors. On the contrary, they intrigue and captivate him, as henceforth they will intrigue and captivate his readers and his contemporaries. Certainly, the romantic trend in stripes is owed neither to Buffon or his *Histoire naturelle*, but the work is clear evidence of a new attitude with regard to them. The rage for stripes can begin.

The origin of this fashion is found among the Americanophiles in France and those countries hostile to England at the end of the 1770s. The American Revolution is itself an offshoot of the Enlightenment, and the flag with the thirteen red and white stripes for the thirteen American colonies, rebelling against the British crown, appears as the image of Liberty and the symbol of new ideas.[51] Likewise, the stripe rapidly acquires an ideological and political status: wearing it, adorning oneself with it, displaying it at home or outside can be a means of proclaiming one's anglophobia or one's support of the movement for freedom. But it is also, quite clearly, a fashion trend, which, as much in France as in the other European countries, spreads rapidly throughout a large segment of society. Even England, originally its direct target, nevertheless adopts the stripe at the end of the 1780s. From then on, everywhere on the old continent there's an unfurling of stripes. Dresses, jackets, jerkins, coats, frock coats, waistcoats, petticoats, blouses,

4. THE ANIMAL STRIPE:
the zebra—"the most elegantly dressed quadruped" (Buffon)
Engraving done for an edition of Histoire naturelle *dating from 1764.*

stockings, pants, trousers, aprons, ribbons, scarves: as much at court as in the villages, most pieces of clothing are, or can be, striped. The aristocratic stripe and the peasant stripe meet up with each other and sometimes merge, as in the country and shepherd scenes of which painters and engravers have left so many examples.

From the domain of clothing, the new fashion in stripes gradually extends to that of fabric for interiors and furniture: drapes, curtains, tapestry, furniture, and sheets of all kinds are covered, in their turn, with this sober and regular decor that breaks with the garlands, the patterns, and the chinoiseries of the preceding period. Because neoclassical taste, as well, favors the expansion of stripes. These latter are thin, vertical, and of brighter or lighter colors than in the sixteenth or seventeenth centuries. Henceforth red-black, blue-white, green-white, and green-yellow combinations dominate. The stripe makes rooms larger, energizes the atmosphere, brightens the surfaces where it appears. In France, in the area of decorative arts, the late Louis XVI style and especially the Directoire style make great use of it.[52]

And it is true, the ideology had, for a few years already, made it into an emblematic image for the Revolution now getting under way.

The Revolutionary Stripe

It is difficult to say precisely why the French Revolution made such wide use of stripes and striped surfaces, to the point where they end up in its emblematic repertoire side by side with the fasces, the pike, the tricolor rosette, the image of Marianne, and the Liberty cap. In 1989, at the time of the commemorative bicentenary, every ceremony, every depiction of the Revolution involved the massive presence of striped objects, clothes, and fabric. Without stripes, no revolutionary atmosphere. For two centuries, in paintings, engravings, picture books, theater, and later in film, television, comic strips, all revolutionary decor is striped decor, and any patriot or sansculotte is a figure wearing striped pants or vest. Is it going too far to see in this a vestige of the image of the devil, juggler, or hangman, three transgressors—like the sansculottes—against the established order? Is it going too far to establish a posteriori a connection, at once dreamlike and geometric, between the bars of the Bastille, those of the prisons of the Reign of Terror, and the striped clothing so prized by the men of the Revolution?

And nevertheless, at the end of the eighteenth century, the stripe is neither a creation nor a monopoly of the French Revolution. We have just seen that it came from America (and, even up to our own times, the "stripes" will retain throughout a certain American connotation) and that, in the old country, it is a style well before 1789. From the outset, it is a matter of a phenomenon going way beyond the framework of France. What's more, in this country, until the proclamation of the Republic, the stripe is worn as much by supporters of the ancien régime as by its adversaries. So where, beginning from this date, does its specific power to proclaim republican, patriotic, and even, sometimes, insurrectional ideology come from?

It comes first from the tricolor rosette and flag. Both of them are, in their own way, striped surfaces, different, of course from classical stripes (tricolor instead of bicolor and a single sequence instead of repeated sequences), but belonging rhythmically to the same value system and the same sensibility. Visually comparable to a target, the rosette is generally made of three concentric stripes (sometimes the sequence is repeated twice); it radiates from its center and seems to put into motion the medium on which it appears. It can be seen from a distance, from a much greater distance than if it were monochrome, and nevertheless it is worn on the person. It is an *insignia* in the full sense of the word.

Adopted by the Parisian insurgents beginning on July 17, 1789—under circumstances and for reasons that are still far from perfectly clear, no matter what La Fayette says in his *Mémoires*[53]—this tricolor rosette quickly becomes the emblem of the national guard and, by extension, is interpreted as an image of the civic unity of the country. Certain patriotic exegetes even see the three colors as an evocation of the three national orders.[54] The celebration of the Federation, July 14, 1790, reinforces this idea and sanctions the deification of tricolor decorations and insignia, among which the rosette occupies first place. At the beginning of the Convention, which renders its use obligatory in many circumstances, it appears as the official, nearly sacred symbol of the new regime. To attempt to remove it or profane it is a crime against the state and the homeland that carries with it extremely severe penalties. To sell other than tricolor rosettes is punishable by death.

The three-colored flag, on the other hand, only later acquires true official status. What's more, in the form that we know it, it is defined, according to a drawing by David, only by a Montagnard Convention decree on February 15, 1794, and this definition takes a certain amount of time to pass from the domain of the law to that of reality. For a few years still, horizontal stripes continue to compete with vertical stripes, and in this latter arrangement, the place nearest the pole is sometimes occupied by the red, sometimes by the blue, sometimes by the white. The definitive formula will have to wait for the Consulate to be imposed.[55]

But, for a long time already, the three colors had become both the emblem and the symbol of revolutionary France. The tricolor symphony is orchestrated beginning from various, chiefly textile, media: rosettes, standards, flags, but also ribbons, sashes (the mayors receive their tricolor sashes from the Assembly beginning in May 1790), plumes, panaches, canopies, tents, hangings, etc. The great consumer of ephemeral decorations, the Revolution gives continual priority to the textile medium. In doing so, the emblematic ideology can link up with the fashion in clothing and transform it into an instrument for propaganda. All the more so because many revolutionaries want to extend the egalitarian ideal into the world of clothing and dream of a single, striped uniform for every citizen. That's why, even if their use predates 1789, the artisan's or the peasant's red and white striped pants and vest, like the blue and white striped skirt and apron of the dressmaker or washerwoman, become veritable "uniforms" serving patriotic ideas after this date. To dress oneself in stripes is not only to offer proof of public spirit, but also to display one's adherence to certain values important to the latest ideological trend. The Revolution grafts new meanings onto the old forms, structures, and colors. A man of the ancien régime according to his hairstyle and clothing, Robespierre probably already wore his famous striped frock coat before 1789. But beginning from 1792, with hardly any modification, it acquires considerable symbolic power.

Thus, from all perspectives, the revolutionary period constitutes an important time in the history of stripes. Not only do stripes spread throughout, but they become diversified and revised. The tricolor vogue, for example, provides them with a three-part arrangement, formerly rare and henceforth common. Fabrics and clothes can be striped

5. THE REVOLUTIONARY STRIPE:
tri-colored tailcoat with buttoned cuffs,
about 1790–95

with three, four, even five colors without losing their fundamental property: rhythm by alternating sequences.

But it is perhaps in the domain of emblems and insignia that this role as catalyst and innovator for the French Revolution was the most profound and long-lasting. Taking over from ancient heraldry, revolutionary emblems helped to spread the use of insignological formulas constructed around bands and stripes. First of all, the blue, white, and red flag became an archetypal model and engendered, in all corners of the world, numerous tricolor imitations, symbols of independence and freedom. Then, the institutions of many states, nearly throughout Europe and the world, adopted striped geometric marks as emblems, easier to use and to reproduce than the old coats of arms with animal or vegetable motifs. The army especially drew heavily from this kind of repertoire. And finally, these striped insignia and emblems spread from the domain of the state and its institutions to that of commercial firms, private establishments, and games and sports. With the French Revolution, the stripe became and remained the mark par excellence.

To this new dimension, the Consulate and the First Empire, those great consumers of insignia and uniforms, added an exotic and ornamental dimension for a few years. This was the great trend in the "return from Egypt" stripes, so prized beginning from 1799–1800, which, once again, combined a Western fashion (here, more precisely, French) with an Oriental (or supposedly Oriental) decor. Of course, the Directoire had widely extended the "romantic" use of stripes in interior decoration, but the first years of the nineteenth century made nearly systematic use of them in France. Thus the stripe partly abandoned clothing to express itself fully on walls and upholstery fabrics. Under the Consulate, it was even considered to be in the very best taste in high society to set up "Egyptian" striped tents at home and take one's meals, sleep, or receive friends in them.[56] Here we encounter an association—between the tent and the stripe—which has traversed the centuries. It is as noticeable in medieval miniatures as on our contemporary beaches. Always and everywhere, the tent—like all materials and objects having something to do with air and wind—maintains a close relationship with the world of the stripe, whether decorative, functional, emblematic, or even imposed by methods of production.[57]

In fact, striped fabric is very much subject to the constraints of weaving methods, and its popularity, in this or that period, in whatever area, using whatever medium, must also be seen in relation to the history of techniques. There is no doubt that the increasing mechanization of thread and cloth production beginning from the 1770s (James Hergreaves's spinning machine, Samuel Crompton's mule-jenny, and then Joseph-Marie Jacquard's loom) helped to expand the use of striped cloth in clothes, furniture, and decoration. Always and everywhere, the technical and the symbolic go hand in hand. At the end of the eighteenth century and the beginning of the nineteenth, the ideology of the stripe fully benefited from the progress of the industrial revolution.

On walls, the fashion in vertical stripes extends long after the fall of the Empire. Drained of all ideological content, and even of all Oriental connotations, it is still very much present during the Restoration and the beginning of the July monarchy. There is a "physical" reason for that: vertical stripes seem to increase volume. With low ceilings and made up of a succession of small rooms, Restoration apartments, like those of the Directoire, make massive use of striped wall coverings. What's more, we must wonder if the horizontal stripes one sometimes sees painted on the walls of the huge rooms in feudal castles didn't already serve an analogous, but opposite, purpose: to diminish the height of the ceiling and give the illusion of a more contained space. Perhaps the medieval eye had already been shaped by culture—because clearly it is a cultural phenomenon, strictly cultural, not biological or physiological, to see, in vertical stripes, motifs that seem to stretch the surfaces on which they appear, and, in horizontal stripes, motifs that seem to produce the opposite effect?[58]

To Stripe and to Punish

The romantic stripe, onto which is abruptly grafted the revolutionary stripe, marks a decisive stage in the history of stripes and striped fabric. Henceforth, not only can textile stripes be vertical as well as horizontal, but they can also, and especially, be taken as something good. The one who wears them on his clothing is no longer necessarily an outcast or a reprobate as was the case in the Middle Ages.

This new quality will survive to the end of romanticism, cross the decades, and endure into our own time. However, for all that, the bad stripe is not going to disappear. On the contrary, what characterizes the contemporary period is the coexistence of two opposing value systems, based on one and the same surface structure. Since the end of the eighteenth century, the stripe can either enhance or detract from one's status or do both at the same time. On the other hand, it is never neutral. The last chapters of this book are devoted to these two value systems. And, so as not to break the established pattern, let's first return to the bad stripe, the one we've seen draw attention to a negative character or nature ever since the feudal period.

In our contemporary imagination, an individual provided with striped clothes can call to mind various professions or social statuses. But the first thing we think of, especially if the stripes are wide and well contrasted, is the status of the prisoner. Certainly, in no Western countries are prisoners so outfitted anymore,[59] but the image of such a costume has remained strong enough to function as an attribute, indeed even as an archetype, for us. The comic strip—discourse in coded and supercoded images—makes no mistake in almost invariably giving a striped tunic or shirt to all ex-convicts, convicts, and prisoner types it represents. For francophone readers, the most well-known example is found in the adventures of Lucky Luke, where, since 1950, the formidable and ridiculous Dalton brothers are perpetually dressed in yellow and black striped shirts. Such a costume is enough to signify that this is a matter of outlaws escaped from prison or hard labor camps. Likewise, advertising, which often uses codes close to those of the comic strips, continues to include images of such figures as well, thus contributing to the perpetuation of an archetype—the prisoner or the convict in striped clothes—that no longer corresponds to reality.

Nevertheless, the true history of striped costumes for prisoners and convicts remains difficult to reconstruct.[60] Here again, the stripes seem to come from America. It was probably in the penal colonies of the New World (Maryland, Pennsylvania) that this costume first appeared, about 1760. It is not impossible, incidentally, that the colonists rebelling against the British crown (and later, the French revolutionaries) deliberately made it the symbolic dress for the uprisings for Liberty. Later on, in the early nineteenth century, we encounter this costume in certain English and German prisons, and then, with the passing decades, in many penal colonies in Austria, Siberia, and even the Ottoman Empire. French penal colonies, on the other hand, never made use of it, preferring to dress convicts in a red tabard rather than a striped tunic.[61] But, in both cases, the intention is the same. As in the Middle Ages, it is a matter of creating a distance in order to emphasize that those who wear such a uniform are excluded from the social order and subject to a separate regime.

This functional equivalence between plain red and bicolor stripes is interesting on several accounts. From the social perspective, its dates are clearly defined: such an equivalence would have been impossible in the Middle Ages, and even still in the sixteenth century, as the color red was too widely worn then to constitute a deviation.[62] From the semiological perspective, on the other hand, it conveys the timeless, nearly absolute link between the color red, stripes, and the bright and gaudy. Here we are in the domain of the garish, the loud, even the dynamic. And all the more so because the red tabard of French convicts is often combined with ochre or brown pants, and sometimes a green cap (for those condemned for life) and because yellow sleeves were often sewn onto it to distinguish the repeat offenders.[63] All prisoners must be seen from a distance, differentiated from the guards, grouped together, and easily spotted if they flee from prison or their place of deportation. The stripe and the multicolor are perfectly suited for doing this. From which stems their equivalence, which, furthermore, we have already encountered many times with regard to the identifying function of stripes in medieval society. I admit, however, that I haven't been able to find a concrete link—material or institutional—that would tie the dress of convicts and deportees of the modern era to that of the outcasts of medieval society. There is no doubt this link exists in the domain of thinking, sensibility, imagination, and in systems of representation. But, in actual practice, how did the modern Western world gradually make striped clothes the specific garb of prisoners? That remains to be studied in detail.[64]

And all the more so because it seems to me that in this category of modern and contemporary stripes there exists a dimension that, is not, or hardly, present at all in medieval stripes. The stripes of convicts and deportees are not only a social mark, the sign of exclusion or of a particular status. Inscribed on cheap cloth, there is something profoundly degrading about them, which seems to take away all dignity and all hope of salvation from the one who wears them. Moreover, combined with disturbing, vulgar, or sullied colors, they themselves often seem charged with evil powers. Not only do they identify and exclude, they degrade, mutilate, carry bad luck. The most telling and most painful example of such stripes remains that of the clothes imposed on death camp deportees by the Nazi concentration camp system. Never have stripes inscribed on the body violated human dignity so profoundly.

Further upstream, madness and internment may be the areas where we must look for a certain continuity between the medieval hallmarks of dress and the garb of modern prisoners. From the clown to the madman and from the madman to the maniac there is no break, but, on the contrary, a tragically coherent course, which could have been the course stripes took as well. The important links here would probably be the confinement of "madmen" beginning in the six-teenth century (in England first, and later on the continent), and then the confinement of all those committing crimes and misdemeanors in the second half of the seventeenth century, when depriving criminals of freedom gradually replaces older forms of corporal punishment.[65] Geometrically and metaphorically, there is a very strong link between the horizontal stripes of penitentiary wear and the vertical stripes that make up the prison bars. Intersecting at right angles, stripes and bars seem to form a web, a grill, even a cage, that isolates the prisoner even more from the exterior world. More than just a mark, here, the stripe is an obstacle. Moreover, it is this same obstacle stripe—very often red and black—that we encounter today at grade crossings, border posts, at all places where it's necessary to stop.

One final domain also helps to highlight the link between the stripe and punishment, exclusion, or privation: the lexicon. In modern French, the verb *rayer*, to stripe, has the double meaning of making stripes and

6. THE CONCENTRATION CAMP STRIPE:
prisoner at Alcatraz, about 1920

of removing, deleting, eliminating. *Rayer* can mean "to strike off" a name on a list, to make a line through it and thus exclude that person from whatever the list allows. Most of the time, this serves as a kind of punishment. The same idea is found again in the verb *corriger*, correct, which means both to stripe and to punish, and which, with the second definition, gives rise to the expression, *maison de correction*, house of correction, a place of confinement where the windows have bars and the prisoners—sometimes—wear stripes. The verb *barrer*, to bar, which is often synonymous with *rayer*, to stripe, underlines very accurately how bars are stripes and stripes are bars.

Similar relationships are found again in German, where the verbs *streifen*, to stripe, and *strafen*, to punish, probably have a common etymology (no matter what the specialized indexes say).[66] They belong to a family of words to which it is possible to link the noun *Strahl*, ray, and maybe the word *Strasse*, street, the street finally being only a particular kind of stripe.[67] In English, the term *stripe*, which refers to striped fabric, must be related to the verb *to strip*, which has the double meaning of undressing and depriving (or even punishing), and the verb *to strike off*, which means to cross out, to bar, to exclude from a list.[68]

Latin is not to be outdone, as it also uses a vocabulary emphasizing the link between the idea of the stripe and that of punishment. Words like *stria* (stripe, streak), *striga* (row, line, furrow), *strigilis* (rake, scraper) belong to the large family of the verb *stringere* which, among its different meanings, includes those of clasping, striping, and depriving, and which, especially, gives rise to the verb *constringere*, meaning literally to imprison.

Whether Latin, English, German, or French, all these words connected by the radical *stri-* emphasize the close kinship between Latin and the Germanic languages in these areas. There is little doubt that they proceed from a shared Indo-European source.[69]

Thus it seems undeniable that, over the very long term, Western culture has associated the idea of the stripe with that of impediment, prohibition, punishment. To stripe is to exclude, and, for a very long time, all those who have worn striped clothes have been outcasts from society. All the same, it is also possible that this exclusion has sometimes been considered not so much a privation of rights or freedom as a protection. The striped costume medieval society gave to fools and the insane is certainly an ignominious mark, a sign of exclusion, but it can also be a barrier, a gate, even a filter that protects them from evil spirits and diabolic creatures. We may find here the obstacle stripe, but not an obstacle stripe having only a negative function. Fragile, defenseless, the madman, more than most, is prey for the devil. So that the insane not become possessed, it is useful, if it isn't too late, to dress him in a protective suit, a costume that serves as filter or barrier: a striped costume. There's no reason not to think that the belief in the protective virtues of such dress stripes has more or less endured into the contemporary era. Aren't our pajamas striped to protect us during the night, while we rest, fragile and pathetic, from all bad dreams and interventions by the devil?[70] Our striped pajamas, our striped sheets, our striped mattresses, aren't they grills, cages? Didn't Freud and his followers ever think of this?

Stripes for the Present Time
(19TH–20TH CENTURIES)

THE HISTORIAN CAN SURMISE, however, that various reasons exist to explain the presence of stripes on nightclothes. There is, in fact, the whole issue of "underclothes," that is, clothes that touch the body, an issue our striped pajamas and night wear pose. Why is such clothing so often decorated with stripes or bands of different colors? What is the source of this custom? Where does it fit in the long and decidedly nonlinear history of striped cloth?

More than the history of hosiery, weaving methods, and cleaning practices, it is social symbolism and dress codes we must call on to attempt to answer these questions. Here, perhaps more than anywhere else, the problem of the stripe is really a problem of color. Examining this briefly in the pages that follow will allow us to leave behind the yoke of pejorative stripes and rediscover the universe of ennobling stripes, glimpsed in the romantic period. But here, it is a matter of stripes of an entirely different nature, no longer posing the question of their appearance in terms of horizontal and vertical but rather in

terms of color and width, and especially posing the question of the social order—always inseparable from the problem of the stripe—from
the perspective of personal hygiene.

Hygiene of the Stripe

For many centuries, from the height of the feudal period until the second industrial revolution, Western sensibility had no tolerance for
clothes and fabrics that touched the body directly (chemises, veils,
breeches, boxer shorts, sheets) being any color but white or ecru.
Sometimes, as in certain monastic regulations, it might be expressly
ordered that these clothes not be dyed, the undyed representing the
zero degree of color even more so than white. Such prescriptions result from color passing for something more or less impure (especially if obtained through animal matter), more or less unnecessary, and
terribly immodest. It had to be kept at a distance from that intimate
and natural surface that constituted the skin. Through the ages, all
Western moral codes on color have agreed on that point, whether
those of the twelfth- and thirteenth-century Cistercian or Franciscan
order (Saint Bernard and Saint Francis are two great enemies of dye-
ing and color), the sumptuary laws of the late Middle Ages, the Protestant Reformation (very much against color), the Catholic Counter-
Reformation (in some way obliged to recoup some of the values of
the Reformation), or, finally, early industrial society which inherited
the Protestant ethic, in this domain as in many others.[71] Thus, from
the eleventh to the nineteenth century, a sheet or chemise could only
be white or undyed.[72]

The earliest changes appeared after 1860, first in the United States
and England, and then in the rest of Europe. Freed from the Protestant

moral code, the capitalist ethic, and bourgeois values, manufacturers and their clientele slowly developed the habit of selling or buying underwear, bathroom linens, sheets, and nightclothes that were not exclusively white or ecru, but "colored."[73] This occurred discretely at first, and then in a more marked fashion directly following World War I. This slow process of passing from white to colors lasted a little over a century and evolved differently according to the categories of textiles and clothes. To wear a sky-blue shirt was unthinkable in 1860 but had become standard by 1920 and, in 1980, constituted the most commonplace event (blue men's shirts having become even more ordinary and more frequently worn than white shirts). On the other hand, to sleep in bright green or red sheets represented an inviolable taboo in 1860, and this was still true not only in 1920 but also in 1960. Ten years later, that was no longer entirely the case, and today, without having become common, examples can be found. Thus for sheets, unlike shirts, there was not a gradual evolution but an acceleration and a stark change over the course of the last twenty years.

Thus the movement from white to color did not take place throughout according to the same rhythm. But everywhere, on all kinds of media, it used the same means: the pastel and the stripe. Indeed, nowhere has there been an abrupt shift from white to bright, saturated colors. There are always intermediate periods, and whether it's for the bed, underwear, bath towels, or nightclothes, these intermediate periods have always been periods of pastels or stripes. Often, in fact, the two converge, the movement toward color taking place in the same period and toward the same ends, whether through the use of pastel or diluted colors, or through the combination (in the form of stripes) of white and one other color, also diluted. In both cases, at the

7. THE HYGIENIC STRIPE:
a pair of women's laced silk stockings,
Great Britain, about 1860–65

beginning of the process, that is, around 1920–40, it was cold colors in particular that were called on for these roles.[74]

It is interesting to note here the nearly grammatical equivalence between the stripe and the pastel within the Western dress system between the end of the nineteenth century and the end of the twentieth (it worked completely differently in other periods and in other cultures). The pastel is a failed color, an almost color, "a color that dare not speak its name."[75] The striped—used in this way—is a half color, a mutilated color, a color woven with white. In both cases, the hue is broken (almost in the heraldic sense of the word), and even though technically very different, these two methods of breaking fulfill the same dual function: to enliven the white and to purify the color. Personal hygiene and the social moral code are safeguarded, all the while permitting emancipation from the long tyranny of white and nondyed fabrics. Furthermore, what occurred with regard to material and clothing sometimes happened in a parallel fashion for other objects related to hygiene, health, and the body. Kitchen and bathroom walls, hospital rooms, swimming pool tiles, household appliances, dishes, toilet articles, packaging for medications: everywhere, the move from hygienic white to enlivening and diversifying color was made through the means either of pastel dyes or striped surfaces.

But let's stay with the domain of textiles and note that the hygienic stripe, offspring of industrial society and thus very far removed from the medieval stripe over which we lingered so long, remains a widespread presence in our everyday world. We still wear striped shirts[76] and underwear; we use striped bath and hand towels; we sleep under striped sheets. The canvas on our mattresses has remained striped. Is it going too far to think that those pastel stripes that touch our bodies not only respond to our worries about keeping clean but also play the role of protecting us? Protecting the body against dirt and pollution, against external attacks, but protecting it also from our own desires, from our irresistible appetite for impurity? Thus once again we may find here the barrier stripes, the filtering stripes mentioned earlier regarding inmates and convicts.

What's patently clear, in any event, is the way society, over the course of the decades, has constructed on these hygienic stripes very elaborate codes. Typical cases in this regard are the shirt and the suit (in the modern sense of the word). A veritable sociocultural semiology of the stripe has been established, classifying individuals and groups according to the striped clothes they wear: wide stripes or narrow stripes, stripes combining white with a bright color or a pastel color, vertical stripes or horizontal stripes, continuous stripes or discontinuous stripes. Some of these stripes are considered vulgar, others in good taste, some are thought to slim down or enliven the figure,[77] others to make it look younger or older. Some stripes are fashionable, others are not. And as so often, as always, in fact, these fashions come and go, reverse themselves, differentiate one social class from another, one country from another. Since the last war, however, a few constants seem to have resisted the force of time and been able to affect a wide sampling of society. For all clothes that touch the body, and even for some exterior clothes, thin and pale stripes get better press than wide ones with violently contrasting colors. Thus both the banker and the gangster wear striped suits and shirts, but it is absolutely not a matter of the same stripes: narrow and discrete in the first case, wide and garish in the second.

These latter are considered vulgar. But, quite clearly, to display a certain vulgarity voluntarily can, according to the circles and the circumstances, sometimes also be "the latest style." Likewise, it seems to have gradually become established that striped clothing has a more masculine than feminine connotation, even if a great number of women wear striped clothes. We sometimes contrast striped masculine decor with patterned feminine decor (which often goes back to the archetypal opposition between the long and the round). But there is nothing systematic about this. If it is unusual to encounter men wearing polka dotted or flowered underwear—this would almost be a transgression—the opposite is not true, because many women wear bras and panties with pretty, delicate, feminine stripes.

Thus all throughout our century, the codes for striped dress have become more and more varied, subtle, and full of nuances. But the hygienic and intimate stripes have clearly not evolved all alone. They join with stripes of a different nature to organize and enrich these codes. Among those other stripes, one occupies a primary position: the maritime stripe.

A World in Navy Blue and White

It isn't easy to determine where and when the use of striped clothing appeared among sailors and seafarers. Nor to figure out how and why.[78] The texts remain silent for a long time on this practice, and the images provide no evidence predating the mid-seventeenth century. Beginning from this date, a few English and Dutch paintings, representing naval battles, begin to show sailors wearing horizontally striped tunics, either red and white, or blue and white. But we must really wait until the end of the next century for examples to become numerous. After that, they multiply, and even similarly striped trousers appear. From then on, for most of the Western seafaring world, regulations of all sorts attest to and codify the close ties that unite the sailor and the stripe system.

The striped shirt is not really worn by all sailors. It belongs exclusively to the world of the seamen, that is, to the simple crew members who participate in maneuvers under the leadership of masters and officers. In eighteenth-century paintings, that shirt already seems to play the role of emblematic dress indicating the crew members, a role it has retained until our own times. Thus this article of clothing relegates the one who wears it to the bottom of the hierarchy and can sometimes be charged with pejorative connotations. Still today, for example, those officers who haven't come out of naval schools but up through the ranks, thus those who formerly wore blue and white striped jerseys, are cruelly labeled by other French navy officers as "zebras."[79]

The historian is entitled to wonder if a relationship exists between the pejorative striped clothes used by medieval society and the first striped dress worn by sailors in the modern period. Does such dress originate with a certain idea of the demeaning mark? Or rather, is it purely and simply a matter of an identifying costume, maneuvers aboard ship always being dangerous and obliging the crewmen to make themselves recognizable under all circumstances? The stripe is always more easily seen than the plain color, especially if that stripe combines red and white, a combination of colors which, in this function, aboard ship, certainly seems to have preceded blue and white.

Could it be, however, that the origin of these maritime stripes is neither ideological nor semiological but simply textilogical? The sailors' striped shirt is, indeed, a jersey, that is, an undershirt holding in warmth and cut from knitted fabric, the making of which is related to hosiery. Now, for a long time, for partly technical reasons, the European hosiery trade produced, above all, striped articles of clothing (stockings, breeches, caps, gloves).[80] Thus must we relate the appearance of the striped jersey among sailors on the cold seas to the distribution of machine-made hosiery beginning from the middle of the seventeenth century? The symbolic history and its long duration might lose something here, but the chronology of the phenomenon would be strengthened.

Whatever the case, since that date, the sailor's stripe has crossed the centuries and the oceans. In representational systems and in actual fact, an attraction, even an assimilation, took place between striped clothing or cloth and the sailors' world. All the more so because on-board ship, stripes are not only present on the bodies of the sailors. Other striped fabric can be found there, beginning with certain sails—descendants of antique and medieval sails, which are nearly always striped[81]—and, for the most part, the flags. Since at least the eighteenth century, these latter follow various signal codes, based on principles closely related to those of heraldry.[82]

Nonetheless, for the historian, that isn't the most remarkable thing; nor even is the adoption of striped clothes by fishermen, yachtsmen, landlubbers, or Venice gondoliers! Most interesting is to follow the nineteenth- and twentieth-century transformation of the stripe of the high seas into the stripe of the seashore, and then into the stripe of sports and leisure. It is a matter of a very large-scale social phenomenon that gradually merged all the old uses of the stripe into a single system and that occupies a place of primary importance in our everyday life today. It deserves a moment's pause.

It is in discovering sea bathing and the pleasures of the beach that European society shifted the maritime stripe from the great open sea to the shore. Unknown in the eighteenth century, rare in the first half of the nineteenth, this trend in striped clothes and fabrics, borrowed from the world of sailors, is already solidly in place on the Normandy coasts by the end of the Second Empire. It never stops expanding over the following decades. Beginning in 1858–60, a painter like Eugène Boudin left us much evidence of it: canvas tents and seats, bathing suits, women's dresses, young women's parasols, children's clothes, all or nearly all are already striped at the seashore.[83] The phenomenon affects the coasts of southwestern France as well, and then, a bit later, those of England and

Belgium. On the eve of World War I, there is no longer a beach in temperate Europe that hasn't become a veritable theater for stripes.[84]

This trend in stripes for swimming cannot be explained simply as a fashion phenomenon. We must look for other reasons beyond fashionable society's simple desire to imitate the dress of a disfavored professional group: sailors. Of course, at the seashore, one is freed from certain constraints, dares to do what wouldn't be done in the city, transgresses certain customs, sometimes even mixes with the riffraff. But one doesn't go there simply for that. One also goes there to breathe the fresh air, bathe, exercise, improve one's health. To frequent seaside resorts in the Belle Epoque is done as much for reasons of health as for fashion.[85] That's why on the beach we once again find the healthy and moral stripes mentioned in the last paragraph. For bourgeois society at the end of the nineteenth century and the beginning of the twentieth, what touches the body must always still be white, pastel, or striped. Thus the beach implements a merger between the stripes of sailors and of moralists.

A typical case in this matter is the bathing suit. Hygienic doctors wanted it to be white. But white, in no matter what fabric, presents the serious inconvenience of being nearly transparent upon leaving the water. Neither can the hygienists prescribe black or dark suits, because to wear a single, dark color directly against the skin in this era is still considered unhealthy. From which derives the fashion in striped swim wear, combining a light color and a dark color, usually white and navy blue. The social moral code and physical purity can thus be upheld, and the hygienic stripe can be merged with the sailors.'

No need to expand much further on the extraordinary diffusion of these "seashore" stripes after the Belle Epoque. The more our century advances, the more stripes invade the beaches: bathing suits and leisure clothes, bathrobes, towels, tents, parasols, wind breaks, deck chairs, shop awnings, children's toys, balls, sports bags, objects and accessories of all sorts. We must wait until the seventies, even the eighties, for the phenomenon to begin to slow down and then to decline. Without disappearing—far from it—striped decor then gradually gives way to other styles, first exotic (trying to evoke tropical beaches and the South Seas), and then "Californian" (adolescents and young people imposing here as everywhere their tastes and fashions).

Before that, between the thirties and the sixties, the proliferation of stripes on the beaches is accompanied by a certain de-aristocracizing. The seaside is no longer visited by only the wealthiest classes; other social groups gradually adopt the habits, customs, codes, fabrics, and clothes of those first vacationers. By spreading, fashions are compromised. Nevertheless, contrary to other kinds of decor, stripes are never proletarianized. Despite mass distribution, especially after World War II, stripes have nearly always retained a reputation for elegance and good taste. The snobbery of the stripe, which seems to have attained its height in about 1900–1920, has certainly disappeared, but for all that, the code hasn't been reversed. As a general rule, to appear on the beach dressed in stripes has often remained more or less "chic." Even if, as we have seen, there are stripes and there are stripes, and even if the slightest deviance from the norms of the moment, as far as the stripe's width, color, or texture is concerned, can relegate its wearer to the most ignominious vulgarity.[86]

The endurance of "chic" stripes is especially a matter of those combining white with one other color. The presence of white seems to confer on them a quality of unfailing neatness and freshness. Moreover, it is the stripe's freshness that we encounter, sometimes very far from the beach, among sellers of perishable products. At the dairy, the fish seller's, the butcher's, the produce seller's, a striped awning or display window always makes a good impression and seems to guarantee the freshness and excellence of what is sold within. As an aside, other shops, which sell no fresh products at all, don't hesitate either to use striped awnings or decor to give themselves an elegant, youthful, gay, and summerlike air.

Because, over the course of the decades, the seaside stripe, having become the stripe of vacations and summer, no longer has only to do with sailors' clothes and bathers' health. It has taken over the world of leisure, of games and sports, of childhood and youth. From being healthy, fashionable, and maritime, it has become playful, athletic, and happy.

Oddball Zebras

The relationship between the child and the stripe is very old. Some medieval pictures already show infants wrapped in strips of cloth forming a striped structure meant to hold on their diapers.[87] Later, under the ancien régime, in aristocratic circles, when striped clothes are the fashion among adults, they are also the fashion for children. The same is true during the Revolution. Many engravings represent little patriots in striped trousers, vests, skirts, or aprons. This evidence remains anecdotal however. It isn't really until the second half of the nineteenth century that a privileged relationship between the world of the stripe and the world of childhood will be established. Since then, it has never stopped developing.

Whether infant or adolescent, the child is probably the figure in contemporary society who most often wears striped clothes. The sailor suit dear to little Proust or young Sartre has completely disappeared, of course, but for a long time now, stripes of another sort have come to take over. The model today is no longer the sailor but the athlete. Two "zebras" from different families, but both having similar trouble integrating into the social order.

Because we must first think of the privileged relationship between the stripe and the child in terms of a social mark. Here again, there is great temptation for the historian to skim over the centuries and to see in the striped clothes of today's children the last vestiges of demeaning or excluding stripes from the medieval period. Like the leper, the juggler, the prostitute, the child is, in many respects, a kind of outcast, and the stripe remains, in the long run, the specific mark of that exclusion. But could that be going too far? And all the more so because striped clothes begin to be widely seen on the bodies of small children in the same period as pastel clothes: in the second half of the nineteenth century. Here again we find the equivalence between the stripe and the pastel, as well as the idea of the hygienic stripe. When they are dressed in white, pink, blue,[88] or stripes, little girls and boys wear clothes that do not sully them. Which, in the last analysis, is the opposite of the medieval stripe!

More than a mark of exclusion—though any mark is a sign of exclusion since it emphasizes belonging to one group and thus not belonging to opposed groups—the nineteenth-century childhood stripe is a mark of hygiene, a guarantee of cleanliness and health. For a long time, moreover, striped clothes will retain a reputation for being less easily soiled than others. An idea obviously false on the chemical and material level but one that doesn't reside completely in the domain of perception. The stripe always plays a trompe-l'oeil role. It shows and hides at the same time, and thus helps to conceal spots. We will speak more about this visual function of the stripe further on.

Healthy and clean, and thus "bourgeois," there is something playful about the children's stripe as well, whether because being worn by children has rendered it so or because the childhood stripe merges with two other categories of stripes that we have already encountered here: first, the leisure, vacation, and seaside stripe; second, the stripe of jugglers, minstrels, and all those who, in one way or another, play. To dress a child in stripes sometimes responds to the desire for a referential nod, a parodic effect, indeed even a disguise. Characteristic in this regard is the sailor suit of our grandparents. It is neat, sensible, "chic," but it is happy, even funny, as well. It is a subtle joke, which prompts sympathy and, if not laughter, as least a certain amusement. Its stripes are cheerful because they are a matter of disguise. Just as the stripes of clowns and public entertainers are cheerful. That a stage star like Coluche used to dress in striped overalls to enliven his sketches isn't a matter of chance. Likewise, it isn't by chance that a character like Obélix, Asterix's companion in the comic strip by that name, wears huge, vertically striped blue and white boxer shorts. In different genres, Coluche and Obélix are both players, "oddball zebras." Now, like Buffon in the eighteenth century, contemporary society feels a tender and sympathetic attraction for the zebra—which, in general, it only sees in books.[89] This is a slightly strange animal, "not like the others," often lively and playful, and, most of all, it seems disguised. Likewise, it always seems young. There are no "old zebras," either literally or figuratively. With adults respectably established in life, wearing cheerful or gaudy stripes would be an eccentricity, conveying the desire to shock or transgress. These

8. THE PLAYFUL STRIPE:
two oddball zebras

kinds of stripes are made for the young, for clowns, for artists. They can appear on clothes but also on other media having to do with childhood, celebrations, and play: candy (think of peppermints), toys, fun fair stalls, circus and theater props.[90]

Thus, today, the children's stripe is completely healthy and serene, playful and dynamic, all qualities that companies depend on for selling products meant for the young and anyone who wants to stay young. The well-known brand of toothpaste, Signal®, constitutes a remarkable example of this use of the stripe for commercial ends. It appeared in the late sixties and was meant primarily for children. This was a matter of white toothpaste coated with red stripes. Coming out of the tube, the effect is magnificent.[91] And totally effective. The presence of stripes emphasizes the hygienic quality of the toothpaste, makes it a sophisticated product, seems to speed up the way it comes out, and at the same time brightens it up, makes it funny and appetizing, and transforms tooth brushing into a totally playful activity. You want to eat this white and red striped toothpaste! In fact, more of it is consumed than ordinary toothpaste. Tubes are emptied more quickly because, with it, brushing teeth is no longer a duty but a pleasure. Thus more toothpaste is applied to the brush. In terms of marketing, the creation of such a product was a stroke of genius. As soon as it was introduced to the market, Signal® toothpaste took a leading position and was then copied by other firms. None of them, however, seem to have attained the success of this pioneer brand, the name itself, Signal®, associated with stripes, constituting a veritable spoken coat of arms: a stripe is first of all and forever signaling.[92]

This is very much the case with the athletic stripe, which wants to be seen from a distance and which shares many of the childhood stripe's characteristics: it is not only a means of signaling, but it is also hygienic (it touches the body), playful, summery, young, and dynamic.[93] Like the child, the athlete, a great user of stripes, is an "oddball zebra," who is situated on the margins of society, where he joins the clown, the itinerant performer, the theater person, and all those who devote themselves to show business. Wearing striped clothes on the sports fields can thus be considered, if not a mark of exclusion, at least a deviation and a disguise. In many ways, the athlete is the wandering minstrel of modern times.

But the athletic stripe has an additional and essential function that only exists very discretely for children and performers: the emblematic function. By using one kind of stripe rather than some other kind, the athlete is located within a team, and this team is attached to a club, a town, a region, or a country. The athletic stripe obeys codes that are closely related to those of coats of arms and flags. In any important competition involving many brightly dressed players—a soccer match, for example, or, better still, the most beautiful spectacle athletics has to offer: the final athletic trials in the Olympics—there is a marked heraldic dimension that recalls the medieval tournaments. On the athletes' shorts and jerseys, a great variety of figures and colors are arrayed, as on the shields and banners of the knights. And these figures are very often made up of stripes—horizontal, vertical, diagonal—recalling the colors of the club or the country. As the knight was dressed in his banner, the athlete is dressed in his flag.[94]

Athletic dress still awaits its historians. It would be nice to have at one's disposal here not only works of synthesis but also diagrammatic catalogues similar to those—prolific to the point of being unsettling—available to historians studying military uniforms. It would also be nice to know why in certain sports (baseball, basketball, ice hockey, boxing) most referees have kept the striped clothing that was theirs from the outset, and why, in other sports, this dress, which effectively distinguishes referees visually from competitors, has been abandoned (soccer and rugby, for example). It would be especially nice to know how, within a given club, stripes and colors are arrayed on the jerseys of different teams (professional, amateur, youth, reserves) for each sport, how they form a system, how they are grafted onto the town symbols, how fans use them, their origin, history, significance. How, for example, "aristocratic" athletic stripes (the sky blue and white of a club like the Racing Club of France), student stripes (the purple and white of the Paris University Club), corporate stripes (ASPTT, ASPP, etc.), military stripes, and workers' stripes relate to one another. Even for a soccer club as prestigious as the Juventus of Turin, which has made its famous vertical black and white stripes triumph on all the playing fields of Europe, nearly all research remains to be conducted. This is all the more regrettable since, for the historian of social signs and codes, sports—a domain where written and represented documentation is abundant—constitutes an exceptionally rich area of investigation.

Striped Surface, Dangerous Surface

Oddball zebras are sometimes nasty customers. Indeed, the stripe represents so heavy an accent, as much from the visual point of view as from the social, that the boundary separating the good stripe from the bad is often vague. On the one side, the sailor, the bather, the athlete, the clown, the child, on the other, the madman, the executioner, the prisoner, the criminal. Between the two, a whole range of characters who partake of both worlds and who have in common being located on the margins of society. The latter know how to play with this poly-semy to foster ambiguity or confusion, especially in recent periods when the meanings of the stripe have become so numerous.

Thus, in the Belle Epoque, among the avant-garde, a certain "rogue" stripe came into play that survived World War I and has even lasted well into the twentieth century. Its preferred expression is a shirt or jersey with wide horizontal stripes and garish colors. Provocative, disturbing, and parodic at the same time, it merges at least three categories of stripes we have already studied: those of convicts, sailors, and athletes.

Because this stripe is particularly masculine. It is, for example, what Guy de Maupassant wears when he goes to row and mix with the riffraff on the shores of the Seine. It is also what impressionist painters often represent to portray working-class men amusing themselves in the waterside open-air cafés and dance halls in the company of the demimonde. Because they attract the eye, because they create a dis-crepancy, because they are musical and kinetic, painters have always been attracted by striped surfaces and materials. Early on, they intro-duced them into their paintings (we have already mentioned exam-ples by Hieronymus Bosch and Pieter Bruegel) and have continued to use them through the course of the centuries, from Carolingian reli-gious painting to the most contemporary abstract art. A few painters have even gone further and made the stripe their clothing or disguise of choice. Such was the case with Picasso, an "oddball zebra" if there ever was one, who never missed an opportunity to exhibit himself in stripes, above and below, and to proclaim loud and clear that to make good paintings you had to "stripe your ass."[95] Equally close to us, in an-other genre, is the case of Daniel Burren, another great iconoclast whose creations have hinged on the theme of the stripe nearly ex-

9. THE STRIPE AND THE ARTIST:
Pablo Picasso in his studio, 1957

clusively for more than twenty years.[96] As in the thirteenth century, stripes continue to cause scandal.

Before analyzing the pictorial and musical function of these contemporary stripes, let us emphasize how the "rogue" stripe of the 1900s is still very much present today in advertising, comic strips, and cartoons. A simple horizontally striped jersey is enough to present a dirty street urchin, a thug, a gangster, or some other character who is disquieting but not necessarily a full-fledged criminal. For a long time, the figure of Filochard in *Pieds nickelés* constituted the archetype for comic strip heroes wearing such striped jerseys.[97] On the other hand, much more menacing is the "Al Capone" stripe that appeared in the twenties and thirties to clothe American gangsters and Mafia godfathers. Even though just as garish, they are no longer horizontal, but vertical, and no longer appear on the shirt or jersey, but on the suit. Film has made this suit into one of the most frequently recurring clothing attributes of the underworld and has contributed to its expansion into many categories of images. In France and Italy, journalistic cartoons and drawings use it almost daily to highlight the doubtful or shady character of this or that political figure. A vulgar suit with wide stripes is enough to collapse the fragile barrier that separates the nation's elected from the dangerous *mafioso*.[98]

Thus the pejorative stripe did not disappear with the end of penal colonies and the triumph of seaside resorts or athletics. It is still very much present in our society, even if this presence makes itself more discrete or more strictly coded than that of the positive stripe. Moreover, its meaning has evolved. It no longer designates the devil, as in the Middle Ages, nor really even a transgression of the social order, as formerly and of late. Henceforth it mainly evokes danger and functions more as a signal than a mark of exclusion. The highway code uses it extensively. Everywhere red and white stripes abound, warning of danger, recommending caution, forbidding this or that access. Caution, workers! Slow, detour, stop, obey: in the street and on the road, these are the kinds of direct and indirect messages all red and white striped signs send us. The combination of these two colors, that of interdiction and that of tolerance, brings out fully here the stripe's ambivalence: it is guide and obstacle at once, filter and gate. In certain cases, it is possible to pass, respecting various constraints; in others, it is imperative to stop. That is so at lowered grade crossings, border posts, or when coming upon a police barricade. All are indicated by a profusion of red and white stripes, which not only can be seen from far off—probably, today, what can be seen from the very farthest off[99]— but also provoke a certain agitation, indeed even a real fear. Behind this kind of stripe, danger always lurks. And, along with danger, authority—danger of another sort—embodied by the police, the state patrol, or the customs officer. A stripe often leads to a uniform, and the uniform to a penalty.

Thus most of these red and white stripes used on traffic signs function as screens. They are some sort of shorthand image for a doorway or a fence that can only be crossed under certain conditions. A simple red and white striped horizontal line placed across the road (which sometimes embodies a grade crossing) has the same effect as a huge gate, which could be striped with the same colors and located in the same place. Here we can discern an essential feature of how the stripe functions: metonymically. The stripe is a structure that infinitely repeats. Whether it appears on a tiny surface or one of great dimensions, its properties remain the same. The part is as good as the whole, the structure takes precedence over the form. From which we get the extraordinary plasticity of the uses for the stripe and, over the course of the centuries, its continual employment as mark, sign, insignia, emblem, attribute, whatever the medium, technique, or context.

The pedestrian crossing, which in our day is no longer studded but formed by alternating bands of white and black similar to a zebra's coat (to the point that Germans have nicknamed their pedestrian crossings *Zebrastreifen*), represents another form of these traffic stripes that have to do with danger, a barrier, prohibition, and permission. It is there one must cross, but it doesn't matter when or how. Stripes on the ground indicate both passage and the difficulty of passage. Alternating empty zones and full zones, they require obedience and precaution, as if there were some danger of falling into the spaces separating the white bands. Here again, it is a matter of a filter, letting the pedestrian's legs pass, but retaining all his attention.

This role of filter is also adopted by other categories of stripes, like those we see on shutters and blinds. Here again, it is a matter of screening while letting pass, of protecting without completely forbidding, of stopping that which is harmful and guiding that which is beneficial. This filtering quality may be one of the stripe's great virtues. We have already analyzed it with regard to bodily hygiene. Striped clothes worn directly against the naked skin protect and purify it. We encounter it nowadays regarding the house: openwork shutters, generally made from lath put together to form stripes, protect the inhabitants, especially those sleeping, from all dangers coming from outside, whether it is a question of noise, cold, wind, prowlers, evil spirits, or the devil himself. Like striped pajamas, striped shutters assure the tranquillity of sleep. This protective function is so important in the traditional farmhouse that, in many regions (Savoy, Tyrol), when the physical structure of the shutters doesn't form stripes, they are painted directly on the wood.[100]

Sometimes excess defeats the purpose of the desired protection. Too many stripes no longer filter danger, but, on the contrary, seem to attract it. Alfred Hitchcock constructed an entire film on this theme, *Spellbound*, released in 1945. It depicts a phobia of stripes and lines felt by a man who suffers from a guilt complex following the death of his younger brother, impaled on a gate while they were playing together as children. Hitchcock enthusiasts don't think very highly of this film, which they consider a "mediocre psychoanalytic melodrama,"[101] but the stripe specialist can only admire the virtuosity with which Uncle Alfred has put into images the obsessional movement of striped forms and figures: the play of shadow and light through a blind, views of grills and rungs, marks on a ski trail, accelerated projection of railway crossings and electric poles seen through the window of a train moving at great speed.[102] Seeing this film, one senses fully how and to what extent the world of stripes can be a disquieting, deadening, alienating world, as a result of repeating the same alternating bichromatic sequences. Any stripe is a rhythm, even a kind of music; and as with all music, beyond the harmony and pleasure of it, it can open into pandemonium, deflagration, and then madness.

From the Trace to the Mark

These connections between the stripe and music are very old, deep, and multifaceted. On the social level, they are expressed first of all by clothing. Already in ancient Rome, musicians wore striped clothes, as later would the minstrels of the feudal period, angel instrumentalists in Gothic painting, or the "jazzmen" of the first half of our century.[103]

10. THE MUSICAL STRIPE:
trouvères and musicians at the court of Heinrich von Meissen,
prince of the Minnesänger
Miniature from Codex Manesse, *northern Switzerland, early
fourteenth century*

The musician is always situated on the fringes of society. There is nothing surprising about seeing him dressed in stripes, like all the outcasts and reprobates we have encountered. Moreover, to play music can only be an invitation to enter into striped decor. A simple musical staff, the strings of a violin or harp, organ pipes, a piano keyboard—aren't these in themselves kinds of stripes?

However, the relationship the stripe builds with music is more intimate, more essential, almost ontological. Fundamentally, the stripe is a *musica*, in the full sense that medieval Latin gives to this extremely rich term, much richer than the French word *musique*. As with *musica*, the stripe is tones, sequences, movements, rhythms, harmonies, proportions, all at once. Like *musica*, it is method, flow, duration, emotion, joy. Both share a common vocabulary: scale, range, tone, degree, line, gradation, gap, interval, etc. Both, especially, are linked to the notion of order, whether it is classification or command.[104] Music establishes an order between man and time. The stripe establishes an order between man and space. Geometric space and social space.

Striped surfaces are rarely found in nature. When man encounters them, he considers them curiosities and sometimes fears them (this is the attitude in the Middle Ages), sometimes admires them (this is our contemporary attitude). That is true with the streaks in certain minerals and vegetables. It is especially true with the coats of many animals like the tiger or the zebra, which, after having been considered terrifying savage beasts, are now taken for the most beautiful in all creation. What formerly prompted fear or disgust henceforth attracts and fascinates.[105] Because it remains the exception.

Actually, the stripe is not really a natural mark but a cultural mark, one that man stamps on his environment, inscribes on objects, imposes on other men. In the landscape, it begins with the ploughshare, followed by the teeth of rakes and the tracks of wheels, and culminating with railways, electric poles, telegraph lines, and highways. Everywhere, the landscape bears the mark of human movement and activity in the form of stripes. On objects, any presence of stripes is not only a mark but also a check. To stripe a surface—as, for example, the edge of airmail envelopes—serves to distinguish it, to point it out, to oppose it or associate it with another surface, and thus to classify it, to keep an eye on it, to verify it, even to censor it. Any stripe is almost a cancellation, in the sense that the post office and stamp collector give to that word. Moreover, it is no accident if, today, all inspection marks—on letters, transportation tickets, entrance tickets, labels, bills—use coded stripes and no longer use punching systems or typographical characters as proof of such inspections. Characteristic in this regard is the case of "bar codes" on products sold in large commercial markets. Labels showing the price expressed in figures have henceforth disappeared, and there are those vertical, parallel bars to replace them.[106]

Displayed on human bodies, stripes fulfill these same functions: to signal, to classify, to check, to establish a hierarchy, whether it is a matter of streaks inscribed directly onto the skin among certain African ethnic groups, striped cloth worn by this or that American or Oceanian population, or even all those dress, heraldic, or flag codes we have discussed regarding Western culture. The stripe is always an instrument of social taxonomy. It places individuals into groups, and those groups into the whole of society.

The comb[107] and the rake, which both create stripes, entirely symbolize that setting-in-order function that the movement from trace to mark symbolizes. To stripe is to make tracks and rank, to inscribe and orient, to mark and organize. It is also to fertilize, because all organization, all orchestration, to return to a musical term, is a factor in creation. The comb, the rake, and the plow, which stripe all they touch, have been symbols of fertility and richness since earliest times. Like the rain, like fingers, other fertility symbols having to do with tracks and stripes. What is striped is not only something marked and classified. It is also something created, constructed, like fabric and all structures imitating fabric, like the plank,[108] the fence, the ladder or shelves; like writing, as well: putting in order knowledge and fields fertile with thought, writing is often only a long succession of lines upon its medium.

From here we can better understand why, over the course of centuries, Western man has never stopped marking with stripes anything bearing some relation to disorder. It was a matter, of course, of signaling this disorder, of protecting oneself from it, of warning, but also of putting it back in order, purifying it, reconstructing it. The striped clothes imposed on madmen and convicts are both grills meant to isolate them from the rest of society and stakes, supports, rectilinear routes meant to put them back "on the right track" and "on the straight and narrow path." The stripe is not disorder; it is a sign of disorder and a means of restoring order. The stripe is not exclusion; it is a mark of exclusion and an attempt at reintegration. In medieval society, those outcasts considered *irredeemable* (pagans, for example) are very rarely required to wear striped clothing. On the other hand, all those for whom there is hope of conversion, like heretics and sometimes Jews or Muslims, may be assigned them.

That said, man proposes and the stripe disposes. Its true nature and function cannot be completely subject to the codes society would like to make it express. In the stripe, there is always something that resists enclosure within systems, something that brings with it distress and confusion, something that "makes disorder." Not only does the stripe show and hide at the same time, but it is altogether the figure and the substance, the finite and the infinite, the part and the whole. By the same token, any striped surface often appears as uncontrollable, nearly indiscernible. Where does it begin? Where does it end? Where is the empty and the full, the opened and the closed, the areas of density and desaturation?[109] Which is the primary level and which the one in front of it? Which is under and which is over? Is the zebra a white animal with black stripes, as the Europeans have so long claimed, or a black animal with white stripes, as the Africans have always recognized it to be?[110]

There is, above all, the visual problem of the stripe.[111] Why, in most cultures, is the stripe seen more distinctly than the plain surface? And why does it operate as a trompe-l'oeil at the same time? Does the eye see what fools it more clearly? As opposed to the plain, the stripe constitutes a deviance, an accent, a mark. But, used alone, it becomes an illusion,[112] disrupts the gaze, seems to flash, to move about, to flee. There is no difference anymore between the structure and the figure. The structure has become the figure, and the figure no longer seems able to be fixed to any base nor even to be inscribed in any Euclidean geometry. The pure stripe no longer stops the eye. It is too effervescent to do that. It clarifies and obscures the view, disturbs the mind, confuses the senses.

Too many stripes can finally drive you mad.

Bibliographic Orientation

This book was born out of frequent contact with images: those of the Middle Ages, which my work as historian leads me to encounter almost daily, and those of our times, in which we all are immersed. It is made up more of impressions and interrogations than of compilations. Indeed, the history of stripes and striped cloth constitutes virgin territory into which no author has yet truly ventured. Thus the bibliography I offer here can only be located on the margins of such a subject. Its sole purpose is to orient the reader who wishes to learn more about this or that question brought up in the preceding pages.

1. The History of Fabrics and Techniques

Bezon, Jean. *Dictionnaire géneral des tissus*. Paris, 1859.

Bril, Jacques. *Origine et symbolisme des productions textiles*. Paris, 1984.

Endreï, Walter. *L'Evolution des techniques du filage et du tissage, du Moyen Age à la révolution industrielle*. Paris, 1968.

Francesco, G. de. "A propos de l'histoire de la tenture murale." *Cahiers Ciba* 1, part 4 (1946): 106–30.

Grass, Milton M. *History of Hosiery*. New York, 1955.

Singer, Charles. *A History of Technology*. 5 vols. Oxford, 1954–58.

2. Iconography and Medieval Symbolism

Erich, Oswald A. *Die Darstellung des Teufels in der Christlichen Kunst*. Berlin, 1931.

Glasenapp, F. *Varia, Rara, Curiosa: Bildnachweise einer Anzahl von Musik-darstellungen aus dem Mittelalter*. Hamburg, 1973.

Hammerstein, Reinhold. *Diabolus in Musica: Studien zur Ikonographie der Musik im Mittelalter*. Berne and Munich, 1974.

Pastoureau, Michel. *Figures et couleurs: Etudes sur la symbolique et la sensibilité médiévales*. Paris, 1986.

———. *Couleurs, images, symboles: Etudes d'histoire et d'anthropologie*. Paris, 1986.

Randall, Lilian M.C. *Images in the Margins of Gothic Manuscripts*. Berkeley, 1966.

Rothes, W. *Jesus Nährvater Joseph in der bildenden Kunst*. Fribourg, 1925.

Schade, Herbert. *Dämonen und Monstren: Gestaltung des Bösens in der Kunst des Frühen Mittelalters*. Ratisbonne, 1962.

Schmidt-Wiegand, Ruth. *Text und Bild in den Codices picturati des Sachsen-spiegels*. Munich, 1986.

3. History of the Carmelite Order

Martini, C. *Der deutsche Karmel*. 2 vols. Bamberg, 1922–26.

Monsignano, E., and J. A. Ximenex, eds. *Bullarium Carmelitanum*. 4 vols. Rome, 1715–68.

Sainte-Marie, Père André de. *L'ordre de Notre-Dame du Mont-Carmel: Etude historique*. Bruges, 1910.

Sainte-Marie, Père Melchior de. "Carmel." In *Dictionnaire d'histoire et de géographie ecclésiastiques*. Vol. 11. Col. 1070–1103. Paris, 1949.

Wessels, G. *Acta capitulorum generalium ordinis Beate Virginis Mariae de Monte Carmelo*. 2 vols. Rome, 1912.

Zimmerman, B. *Monumenta historiae Carmelitanae*. Rome, 1907.

4. Outcasts and Systems of Exclusion

Bauer, M. *Die Dirne und ihr Anhang in der deutschen Vergangenheit*. Berlin, 1912.

Bourdet-Pleville, M. *Des galériens, des forèats et des bagnards*. Paris, 1957.

Danckert, Werner. *Unehrliche Leute: Die verfemten Berufe*. Berne and Munich, 1963.

Gross, Angelika. *"La Folie": Wahnsinn und Narrheit im spätmittelalterlichen Text und Bild*. Heidelburg, 1990.

Hampe, T. *Die fahrenden Leute*. 2nd ed. Iéna, 1924.

Hartung, W. *Die Spielleute: Eine Randgruppe in de Gesellschaft des Mittelalters*. Wiesbaden, 1982.

Heinemann, Franz. *Der Richter und die Richtspflege in der deutschen Vergangenheit*. Leipzig, 1900.

Keller, A. *Der Scharfrichter in der deutschen Kultergeschichte*. Bonn and Leipzig, 1921.

Le Clère, Marcel. *La Vie quotidienne dans les bagnes*. Paris, 1973.

Le Goff, Jacques. "Métiers licites et métiers illicites dans l'Occident médiéval." Reprinted in *Pour un autre Moyen Age*, pp. 91–107. Paris, 1977.

Martin, J., and A. Nitschke, eds. *Zur Sozialgeschichte der Kindheit*. Fribourg and Munich, 1986.

Meyer, C. *Die unehrlichen Leute in älterer Zeit*. Hamburg, 1894.

Rossiaud, Jacques. *La Prostitution médiévale*. Paris, 1988.

Salmen, W. *Der fahrende Musiker im europäischen Mittelalter*. Kassel, 1961.

Welsford, Enid. *The Fool: His Social and Literary History.* London, 1935.

Willeford, William. *The Fool and His Scepter: A Study in Clowns and Jesters and Their Audience.* Evanston, 1969.

5. The History of Clothing

Boehn, Max von. *Das Bühnenkostüm in Altertum, Mittelalter and Neuzeit.* Berlin, 1921.

Eisenbart, Liselotte C. *Kleiderordnungen der deutschen Städte zwischen 1350 und 1700.* Göttingen, 1962.

Kitchens, M. *When Underwear Counted, Being the Evolution of Underclothes.* Talladega (USA), 1931.

Mertens, Veronika. *Mi-Parti als Zeichen: Zur Bedeutung von geteiltem Kleid und geteilter Gestalt in der Ständetracht, in literarischen und bildnerischen Quellen, sowie im Fastnachtbrauch, vom Mittelalter zur Gegenwart.* Remscheid, 1983.

Pellegrin, Nicole. *Les V—tements de la Liberté: Abécédaire des practiques vestimentaires franèaises de 1780 à 1800.* Paris, 1989.

Perrot, Philippe. *Les Dessus et les dessous de la bourgeoisie.* Paris, 1984.

Roche, Daniel. *La Culture des apparences: Une histoire du v—tement, XVIIe-XVIIe siècles.* Paris, 1989.

Schidrowitz, Leo. *Sittengeschichte des Intimen: Bett, Korsett, Hemd, Hose, Bad, Abtritt.* Vienna, 1926.

Schwedt, Herbert, and Elke Schwedt. *Malerei auf Narrenkleidern.* Stuttgart, 1975.

Willet, C., and P. Cunnington. *The History of Underclothes.* London, 1951.

6. Bodily Hygiene and Sea Bathing

Anderson, Janice, and Edmund Swinglehurst. *The Victorian and Edwardian Seaside.* London, 1978.

Désert, Gabriel. *La Vie quotidienne sur les plages normandes, du Second Empire aux années folles*. Paris, 1983.

Hern, Anthony. *The Seaside Holiday: The History of the English Seaside Resort*. London, 1967.

Renoy, Georges. *Bains de mer au temps des maillots rayés*. Brussels, 1976.

Stokes, H. G. *The Very First History of the English Seaside*. London, 1947.

Vigarello, Georges. *Le Propre et le sale: L'hygiene du corps depuis le Moyen Age*. Rev. ed. Paris, 1985.

7. Heraldry, Emblems, Flags

Cook, Andrea. *A History of the English Turf*. 3 vols. London, 1901–1904.

Foras, Amédee de. *Le Blason: Dictionnaire and remarques*. Grenoble, 1883.

Neubecker, Ottfried. *Fahnen und Flaggen*. Leipzig, 1939.

Pastoureau, Michel. "Du vague des drapeaux." *Le Genre humain* 20 (1989): 119–34.

———. *Traité d'héraldique*. Paris, 1979.

Rabbow, Arnold. *Lexikon politischer Symbole*. Munich, 1970.

———. *Visuelle Symbole als Erscheinung der nicht-verbalen Publizistik*. Münster, 1968.

Smith, Whitney. *Flags through the Ages and across the World*. Maidenhead (USA), 1975.

8. Sailors and Seamen; Military Matters

Barraclough, E.M.C. *Yacht Flags and Ensigns*. London, 1951.

Bulletin officiel de la marine nationale. Vol. 38: *Uniformes, tenues et insignes des personnels militaires de l'armée de mer*. Paris, 1958.

Dickens, Gerald. *The Dress of the British Sailor*. London, 1957.

Hugo, Abel. *La France militaire: Histoire des armées franèaises de terre et de mer de 1792 à 1837*. Paris, 1838.

Katcher, Philipp R.N. *Encyclopaedia of British, Provincial, and German Army Units, 1775–1783.* Harrisburg, 1973.

Lovette, Leland P. *Naval Customs, Traditions, and Usages.* Annapolis, 1939.

Moeller, Hans Michael. *Das Regiment der Landsknechte.* Wiesbaden, 1976.

Mollo, John, and Malcolm McGregor. *Uniforms of the American Revolution.* London, 1975.

Stoecklein, Hans. *Der deutsche Nation Landsknecht.* Leipzig, 1935.

Swinburne, Henry Lawrence. *The Royal Navy.* London, 1907.

Tily, James C. *Uniforms of the United States Navy.* New York, 1964.

About the Author

Born in 1947, Michel Pastoureau is paleographer/archivist and director of studies at the *Ecole practique des hautes études* (Sorbonne, IVe Section), where, since 1983, he holds the chair in the history of Western symbolism. His first works were devoted to the study of emblems and systems of representation (coats of arms, seals, medals, iconography). His present research deals with the history of animals and vegetables, on the one hand, and the history of the relationship between humans and color, on the other.

Notes

1. This is what the twenty-second chapter of Deuteronomy expressly pre-
   scribes: *Non indueris vestimento, quod ex lana linoque contextum est* (you
   will not wear a garment that is woven of wool and of linen) (Deuteronomy 22.11).
2. The semiology of the stripe is only considered in the present study in so
   far as it concerns social stakes. It goes without saying that the structural
   analysis that could be done ought to be pushed much further. That will
   be the subject of a future work.
3. The small number of images really doesn't allow me long expositions
   and led me to prefer a statement of synthesis to a detailed, analytic
   study of whole groups of cases. It seemed to me that, at first, on such un-
   cleared ground, that was the best approach. But, here again, I hope some
   day to be able to devote a large book of images to the problem of the
   stripe and striped surfaces.
4. The trademark for Adidas sport articles was no mistake, the company
   having chosen for its emblem three parallel bands, shown as stripes on

the clothes and shoes it sells practically throughout the world. These three bands fully connote the idea of speed and athletic performance.

5. No recent synthesis on the history of the Carmelites exists. The work of Father André of Sainte-Marie, *L'Ordre Notre-Dame du Mont-Carmel. Etude historique* (Brussels, 1910), has still not been replaced. However, the article by Father Melchoir of Sainte-Marie, "Carmel," in the *Dictionnaire d'histoire et de géographie ecclésiastique*, vol. 11 (Paris, 1949), cols. 1070–1103, is worth reading.

6. It is probably the idea of a *crooked* figure that links the bar in heraldry—a patch which, in the shield, descends diagonally from right to left—to the idea of illegitimacy. See L. Bouly de Lesdain, "Les brisures d'après les sceaux," in *Archives héraldique suisses*, vol. 10 (1896), esp. 124–28; J. Woodward and G. Burnett, *A Treatise on Heraldry British and Foreign*, 2nd ed. (London, 1896), pp. 542–82; R. Mathieu, *Le Système héraldique français* (Paris, 1946), pp. 115–23; M. Pastoureau, *Traité d'héraldique* (Paris, 1979), pp. 186–87. On the problems of interpretation posed by the ancient meaning of the heraldic term *barre*, see G. J. Brault, *Early Blazon: Heraldic Terminology in the Twelfth and Thirteenth Centuries* (Oxford, 1972), pp. 116–17.

7. The immense record on Franciscan dress and the excesses toward which it led certain monks at the end of the thirteenth century and throughout the fourteenth nevertheless emphasizes the link between what is striped and what is patched or threadbare. Already, in old and middle French, the verb *rayer* (to stripe) can have the meaning of *gâter* (to spoil) or *abïmer* (to damage), and a diversity of colors can be thought of as the mark of extreme poverty or wear. According to a bull dated 1336, Pope Benoît XII thus orders the king of Naples to expel from his realm the "fraticelle" brothers, proponents of an absolute poverty, notably in the area of dress: ". . . *quidam perversi homines, se fratres de paupere vita et aliis nominibus appelantes, qui diversorum colorum seu petiarum vari-*

arum curtos et deformes gestant vestes . . ." On the disputes concerning poverty within the Franciscan order, see D. Lambert, *Franciscan Poverty* (London, 1961), as well as the relevant chapters in the work of F. de Sessevalle, *Histoire générale de l'ordre de saint Franèois: le Moyen Age*, 2 vols. (Brussels, 1940).

8. E. Faral and J. Bastin, *OEuvres complètes de Rutebeuf*, vol. 1 (Paris, 1959), p. 324. Rutebeuf goes on to say that the Carmelites are "fat and square" and that the Beguines have "tender flesh." The two convents were situated where the Celestine barracks stand today, on the right bank of the Seine, in the Arsenal quarter. In a few large towns, it is possible that the "*rue des Barres*," a very common place name, is an old "*rue des Barrés*" ("street of the Barred") or "*rue des Frères-Barrés*" ("street of the Barred Brothers").

9. E. Monsignano and J. A. Ximenez, *Bullarium Carmelitanum*, vol. 1 (Rome, 1715), cols. 35b–37a, 45b–46a; G. Wessels, *Acta capitulorum generalium ordinis Beate Virginis Mariae de Monte Carmelo*, vol. 1 (Rome, 1912), p. 8.

10. See, for example, Father Zimmermann's explanation of this subject in his article, "Les réformes de l'ordre du Carmel," *Etudes carmelitaines* 19/2 (October 1934): 155–95.

11. Among the titles in a vast bibliography, see L. Trichet, *Le Costume du clergé* (Paris, 1986), pp. 72–73.

12. Rouen, archives départemental de la Seine-Maritime, G. 1885, pièce no. 4. I thank my friend Claudia Rabel for having pointed out this document and transcribing it for me.

13. The laity are often of the same opinion when they speak of clerical clothing. In his *Coutumes du Beauvaisis*, Philippe de Beaumanoir, in about 1280, already proclaimed loudly and strongly: "It doesn't befit a cleric to be dressed in a striped robe" (vol.1, chap. 10, §43, édition Beugnot (Paris, 1842), p. 173.

14 W. Koschorreck, ed., *Der Sachsenspiegel in Bildern* (Frankfurt am Main,

1977), plate 94. See the commentary by R. Sprandel, "*Die Diskrimierrung der Unehelichen Kinder im Mittelater*," in J. Martin and A. Nitschke, *Zur Sozialgeschichte der Kindheit* (Munich, 1986), p. 492 n. 18. I thank my friend, Jean-Claude Schmitt, for informing me of this interesting reference.

15. Among a great number of works, I am referring here especially to J. Bumke, *Höfische Kultur: Literatur und Gesellschaft im hohen Mittelalter*, 4th ed., vol. 1 (Munich, 1987), pp. 172–210; and vol. 2, pp. 821–23 (important bibliography); as well as the older work of A. Schultz cited in note 41 below.

16. Nonetheless, see L. C. Eisenbart, *Kleiderordnungen der deutschen Städte zwischen 1350 und 1700*, (Göttingen, 1962); D. O. Hugues, "Sumptuary Laws and Social Relations in Renaissance Italy," in J. Bossy, ed., *Disputes and Settlements: Law and Human Relations in the West* (Cambridge, 1983), pp. 69–99.

17. With all my heart, I call for some new works on the marks of infamy imposed on Jews and Muslims in the medieval Western world. On very many points, our knowledge remains deficient and contradictory. The old work by Ulysse Robert, *Les Signes de l'infamie au Moyen Age* (Paris, 1891) is totally dated today. It clearly seems useless to search for a system of marks of exclusion or infamy common throughout Christiandom. Between the twelfth and fifteenth centuries, there are innumerable variants from one region to another, from one town to another, from one period to another. Moreover, these marks do not exist throughout and, where they do exist, they are neither imposed nor worn in all periods.

18. M. Pastoureau, "Figures et couleurs péjoratives en héraldique médiévale," in *Communicaciones al XV congreso de las ciencias genealogica y heraldica* (Madrid, September 19–26, 1982), vol. 3 (Madrid, 1983), pp. 293–309. Also see the studies collected in proceedings from the colloquium *Exclus et Systèmes d'exclusion dans la littérature et la civilisation médiévales* (Aix-en-Provence, 1978) (*Senefiance*, vol. 5).

19. On the biblical traitors in medieval iconography, see R. Mellinkoff, "Judas's

hair and the Jews," *Journal of Jewish Art* 9 (1983): 31–46; M. Pastoureau, "Tous les gauchers sont roux," *Le Genre humain* 16–17 (1988): 343–54.

20. *Parti* refers to two-colored dress, divided vertically in two halves of different colors. Sometimes the left sleeve is the same color as the right part, and vice versa. Such dress is often equivalent to or a variation of striped dress in the iconography and in medieval society. On this type of clothing, see the thesis by V. Mertens, "Mi-parti als Zeichen: Zur Bedeutung von geteiltem Kleid and geteilter Gestalt in der Ständetracht, in literatrischen und bildnerischen Quellen sowie im Fastnachbrauch, vom Mittelater bis zur Gegenwart, Remscheid," (Germany, 1983).

21. See, for example, what Louis-Sébastien Mercier says on this in his *Tableau de Paris*, vol. 3 (Paris, 1783), p. 138.

22. On the iconography of Saint Joseph, see the extensive note that G. Kaster devotes to him in the *Lexikon der Christlichen Ikonographie*, vol. 8 (Fribourg en Brisgau, 1974), cols. 210–21.

23. J. De Coo, "In Josephs Hosen Jhesus ghewonden wart," *Aachener Kunstblätter* 30 (1965): 144–84; idem, "Das Josephhosen-Motiv in Weinachtslied und in der bildenden Kunst," *Jahrbuch für Volksliedforschung* 11 (1966): 58–89.

24. On French arms and patterned decor in medieval sensibility, see M. Pastoureau, "Le roi des lis: Emblèmes dynastiques et symboles royaux," in Archives nationales, *Corpus des sceaux franèais du Moyen Age. Tome II. Les Sceaux royaux* (by M. Dallas) (Paris, 1991), pp. 35–54.

25. O. A. Erich, *Die Darstellung des Teufels in der Christlichen Kunst* (Berlin, 1931); M. Pastoureau, "Bestiaire du Christ, bestiaire du Diable: Attribut animal et mise en scène du divin dans l'image médiévale," in *Couleurs, images, symboles* (Paris, 1989), pp. 85–110. The problem of freckles is linked in part to that of spots. To be redheaded, to have skin covered with spots, or to wear striped clothes is nearly always experienced in the Middle Ages as some degree or sign of negative status or destiny.

26. C. de Tolnay and P. Bianconi, *Tout l'oeuvre peint de Bruegel l'Ancien*, plate (Paris, 1968); F. Grossmann, *Pieter Brueghel: Complete Edition of the Paintings* (London, 1974).

27. I hope soon to be able to devote an in-depth study to the semantic field of the words *varius* and *diversus* in classic and medieval Latin. As a general rule, visually *varius* evokes a variety of superimpositions (with centripetal tendencies); and *diversus*, a diversity of juxtapositions (with centrifugal tendencies). What is spotted is a matter of the *varietas* and not of the *diversitas*. What is striped, on the other hand, is a matter of both simultaneously. Here again, the striped seems like a superlative form of the spotted. On the etymology and rich lexical field of *varius* and *diversus*, see A. Ernout and A. Meillet, *Dictionnaire étymologique de la langue latine*, 4th ed. (Paris, 1959), pp. 713–14, 725–26 (*verto*).

28. The bad name given to the leopard in the twelfth and thirteenth centuries allows the lion to unload on the leopard all its own negative aspects, and thus be prepared for its definitive coronation as king of the beasts in Western culture. See M. Pastoureau, "Quel est le roi des animaux?" in *Le Monde animal et ses représentations au Moyen Age (XI e-XV es.). Actes du XV e Congrès de la Société des historiens médiévistes de l'enseignement supérieur public (Toulouse, 25–26 mai 1984)* (Toulouse, 1985), pp. 133–42.

29. See the texts compiled by C. Gessner, *Historia animalium: Liber primus de quadrupedibus viviparis* (Zurich, 1551), pp. 784–85. On the interesting confusion that the encyclopedist Vincent de Beauvais seems to make between the zebra and the onager, in the middle of the thirteenth century, see his *Speculum naturale*, book 19, chap. 95 (*de diversis generibus onagrorum*), in the edition printed in Douai, 1624, cols. 1434–35.

30. See the numerous examples presented by A. Ott, *Etude sur les couleurs en vieux français* (Paris, 1899), passim. Also see the wonderful study by A.-M. Bautier, "Contribution à l'histoire du cheval au Moyen Age," *Bulletin philologique et historique du Comité des travaux historiques et scien-*

tifiques (1976): 209–49; (1978): 9–75. On the devaluing of striped or spotted cattle in biblical culture, see Genesis 30.25–43.

31. Although expanding, the bibliography devoted to the beast of Gévaudan is often disappointing. See, especially, F. Fabre, *La B—te de Gévaudan en Auvergne* (Saint-Flour, 1901); X. Pic, *La B—te qui mangeait le monde en pays de Gévaudan et d'Auvergne* (Paris, 1971); and Abbé Pourcher, *Histoire de la b—te de Gévaudan, véritable fléau de Dieu* (Mende, 1889). Concerning this subject, see the prints reproduced in D. Bernard, *L'Homme et le loup* (Paris, 1981), pp. 48–57.

32. At the end of the eighteenth century and in the first half of the nineteenth, Germay also experienced its "beasts of Gévaudan." Furthermore, in England and France since the last war, there have been many apparitions of "mystery felines" (V. Campion-Vincent's expression), bearing certain ressemblances to "the beast" and sometimes having striped coats. A colloquium organized by the CNRS (Centre national de la recherche scientifique) and devoted to these appearances was held in Paris in November 1990.

33. On the medieval prostitute and her clothing, see M. Bauer, *Die Dirne und ihr Anhang in der deutschen Vergangenheit* (Berlin, 1912); and J. Rossiaud, *La Prostitution médiévale* (Paris, 1988). From the abundant literature on jugglers' and musicians' clothes, see M. von Boehn, *Das Bühnenkostüm im Altertum, Mittelalter und Neuzeit* (Berlin, 1921); W. Salmen, *Der fahrende Musiker in europäischen Mittelalter* (Kassel, 1961); R. Hammerstein, *Diabolus in Musica: Studien zur Ikonographie der Musik im Mittelalter* (Berne, 1974); and W. Hartung, *Die Spielleute: Eine Randgruppe in der Gesellschaft des Mittelaters* (Wiesbaden, 1982).

34. I will return to this later. What is spotted necessitates two planes; what is striped, in certain cases, necessitates only one.

35. Allow me to refer here to my own works on the origin and spread of coats of arms, especially to my *Traité d'héraldique* (Paris, 1979), pp. 20–58,

which can be supplemented with the articles I compiled in *L'Hermine et le sinople: Etudes d'héraldique médiévale* (Paris, 1982).

36. V. Cereceda, "Sémiologie des tissus andins," *Annales ESC* (1978): 1017–35. Also see Y. Delaporte, "Le signe vestimentaire," *L'Homme* 20, no. 3: 109–42.

37. T. Innes of Learney, *Tartans of the Clans of Scotland*, 5th ed. (London, 1949); F. Adam, *Clans, Septs, and Regiments of the Scottish Highlands* (London, 1952). Let us note in passing that there are no striped tartans; they are all checked.

38. See my articles cited in notes 18 and 25 above.

39. A legend that appeared early (it is already recorded in the thirteenth century) explains the origins of such coats of arms: the count of Barcelona, ancestor of the Aragonese kings, had an entirely gold shield for a coat of arms. Aiding Charlemagne in his struggle against the Saracens (sometimes it's a matter of Charles le Chauve and a battle against the Normands), he was mortally wounded. Having come to attend him in his last moments, the emperor drenched his fingers in the wounds of the dying man and traced on his gold shield five vertical red bands to preserve the memory of that glorious death. This legend appears widely until the seventeenth century in all the treatises on the blazon. In fact, the Aragon kings' arms, which are often emblazoned *d'or à quatre* (and not five) *pals de gueules*, have a Burgundian-Provençal origin, linked to the feudal history of the Arles realm. See M. Pastoureau, "L'origine suisse des armoiries du royaume d'Aragon," *Archives héraldiques suisses* (1980): 3–10. But this legend underlines, in an exemplary fashion, how, in matters of stripes, one can easily move from the *trace* to the *mark*, how almost any *trace* is transformed into a *mark*.

40. In Roman theater, servants and porters are sometimes given striped or multicolored clothes, similar to those of clowns, mimes, or effeminates. Besides the old work by M. von Boehn, cited in note 33 above, see J. André,

Etude sur les termes de couleur dans la langue latine (Paris, 1949), pp. 149–50, 295–96.

41. There are countless textual and representational examples, many examined or cited in the thesis by V. Mertens (see note 20 above), as well as in A. Schultz, *Deutsches Leben im XIV. and XV. Jahrhundert* (Leipzig, 1892). It is in southern Germany, in the Tyrol, and in eastern Switzerland that this practice of striped clothes for domestic officers seems to continue longest into the modern period.

42. See note 20 above.

43. C. Verlinden, *L'Esclavage dans l'Europe médiévale. Tome II. Italie, colonies italiennes du Levant, Levant latin, Empire byzantin* (Gand, 1977); M. Mollat and J. Devisse, *L'Image du Noir dans l'art occidental*, vol. 2 (Fribourg, 1979), pp. 137–60.

44. Works on the iconography of the wise men are numerous and often of high quality. A summary of them can be found in the notice *Drei Könige* published by A. Weis in *Lexikon der Christlichen Ikonographie*, vol. 1 (Fribourg en Brisgau, 1968), cols. 539–49. On the black king in striped clothes, see Mollat and Devisse, *L'Image du Noir dans l'art occidental*, pp. 172–85. One of the most spectacular examples can be seen on the central panel of an *Adoration of the Magi* attributed to Hans Baldung Grien and dating from 1507 (Berlin, Gemäldegalerie).

45. Let us recall that, in most medieval images, Saint John the Baptist, wild man par excellence, wears a striped cloak or striped clothing, evoking his outfit made of a mixure of goat hair and camel hair. Here again, the stripe is grafted onto the idea of mixing.

46. See, for example, the curious catalogue by F. T. Prewett, *The West End: Hand-Book of Liveries* (London, 1895).

47. There is much documentation (chronicles, sumptuary laws, decrees on dress) that attests to the scandal prompted by this new style of *vestes virgulatae*. While awaiting the publication of Odile Blanc's thesis on

clothing at the end of the Middle Ages, a thesis that devotes one chapter (*Enormis novitas*) to this problem of scandal arising in about 1340–60, we may reread the texts published by A. Schultz, *Deutsches Leben im XIV. and XV. Jahrhundert*, passim. Also see the works cited in note 16 above.

48. The great reformers legislated much with regard to dress and constantly recommended wearing somber, serious, and dignified clothing. Their aversion to lively or multicolored clothes extended to striped apparel. See my study, "L'Eglise et la couleur des origines à la Réforme," in *Bibliothèque de l'Ecole des chartes*, vol. 147 (1989): 203–30.

49. Mertens, "Mi-parti als Zeichen," pp. 30–37. Also see H. M. Möller, *Das Regiment der Landsknechte* (Wiesbaden, 1976); and H. Stöcklein, *Der deutsche Nation Landsknecht* (Leipzig, 1935).

50. G. L. de Buffon, *Histoire naturelle*, 3rd ed., vol. 12 (Paris, 1769), pp. 323–24.

51. It is possible that the American revolutionaries had chosen striped cloth, symbol of *slavery* (already in 1770, the prisoners in Pennsylvania and Maryland penitentiaries wore striped clothes), to express the idea of the serf who breaks his chains, and, by the same token, to reverse the code of the stripe: stripes, a sign of the loss of freedom, become, with the American Revolution, a sign of freedom gained. On the (confused) origin of the American flag, the "stars and stripes," see W. Smith, *The Flag Book of the United States* (New York, 1975).

52. H. Clouzot and C. Follet, *Histoire du papier peint en France* (Paris, 1935); "Trois siècles de papiers peints," Exposition at the Musée des Arts Décoratifs, Paris, 1967.

53. The origin of France's tricolor flag remains poorly understood and much debated. If it is patently obvious that the rosette preceded the flag, it is not easy to say how the former emerged between July 14 and 17, 1789, nor, especially, to figure out what the white, blue, and red originally signified. The old explanation (white = the color of the king, blue and red = the col-

ors of Paris) seems to have to be abandoned today. On the eve of the Revolution, Paris had long since given up using blue and red as emblematic municipal colors. As for La Fayette, who is often praised for having established the three colors before July 17, 1789, by endowing the newly created national guard (for whom he was commander) with a specific emblem (rosette of the king and bicolor ribbon of the Parisian militia), he is a great inventor. What seems certain to me is that the three colors are inherited from the American Revolution, because, when the French Revolution breaks out, these colors are already very much the colors of Liberty. Hervé Pinoteau, who is just now finishing a work on *Les Symboles de la France*, shares this opinion. Nevertheless, see R. Girardet's different view in "Les trois couleurs," in P. Nora, ed., *Les Lieux de mémoire*, vol. 1 (Paris, 1984), pp. 5–35.

54. Still in 1848, Louis Blanc, advocate of the red flag, criticizes the tricolor flag for being an image of a society with classes and contrary to the principle of equality so dear to the Republic. See M. Agulhon, *Marianne au combat* (Paris, 1979), pp. 85–87.

55. See Raoul Girardet's study, cited in note 53 above, which plots out the evolution of the early forms of the tricolor flag. See, too, C. Hacks and G. Linares, *Histoire du drapeau franèais* (Paris, 1934), which replaces D. Lacroix, *Histoire anecdotique du drapeau français* (Paris, 1876).

56. See Jean-Marcel Humbert's wonderful thesis, *L'Egyptomanie dans l'art occidental* (Courbevoie, 1989).

57. All materials filled by wind are or can be striped: tents, sails, pavilions, banners, flags, wind screens, kites, etc. A striped fabric is never totally static; it inflates and deflates, comes to life, changes place, marks a *transitus*—which explains its frequent use in nomination ceremonies and rites of passage.

58. Contemporary dress has turned this kind of cultural practice into a visual system. A heavy man or woman never wears horizontal stripes, which

seem to shorten and thicken the profile, but, on the contrary, seek out vertical stripes, which seem to make one slimmer, especially if those vertical stripes are narrow.

59. In the Soviet Union, on the other hand, such clothes were still worn in the Gulag until very recently (at least if we are to believe certain photographs published by the Western press).

60. I confess to not being able to ascertain the origins of this costume nor its evolution until the mid-nineteenth century. It's true that the bibliography on this subject is extremely limited.

61. M. Bourdet-Pleville, *Des galériens, des forèats et des bagnards* (Paris, 1957), p. 128; M. Le Clère, *La Vie quotidienne dans les bagnes* (Paris, 1973), pp. 118–19.

62. In the seventeenth century, on the other hand, red is ripe, if you'll allow me, for creating this distinction and finding its place on the clothing of outcasts and the condemned, as, for example, on the tabards of galley slaves. Aboard the galleys, on the other hand, striped clothes weren't worn. See A. Zysberg, *Marseille au temps des galères* (Paris, 1983); idem, *Les Galériens du roi: vie et destins de 60,000 forèats sur les galères de France* (Paris, 1987).

63. Besides the works cited in note 61 above, see M. Alhoy, *Les Bagnes: Histoire, types and moeurs* (Paris, 1845); J. Destrem, *Les Déportations du Consulat et de l'Empire* (Paris, 1885); E. Dieudonné, *La Vie des forèats* (Paris, 1932); and P. Zaccone, *Histoire des bagnes depuis leur création* (Paris, 1873).

64. Did sailing—with the exception of the galleys—play a role in this area? From the sailor to the mutineer and from the mutineer to the deportee, these are easy steps to take. For France—although the French navy uses stripes less and later than the English or Dutch navy—see a few comments on the order of dress in A. Cabantous, *La Vergue et les fers: Mutins et déserteurs dans la marine de l'ancienne France (XVIIe–XVIIIe s.)* (Paris, 1984).

65. Here I am obviously referring to Michel Foucault's work, especially *Histoire de la folie à l'âge classique* (Paris, 1961); and *Surveiller et punir: Nais-*

sance de la prison (Paris, 1975). The title of the present chapter is inspired by the title of that latter work.

66. This opinion is not shared by philologists or by any etymological dictionaries of the German language. The latter link the word *Streifen* to the radical *ster-* (as in *Stern*) and to the idea of expanding, spreading, scattering, and not to the large family of the verb *strafen*, to punish. See, for example, L. Mackensen, *Ursprung der Wörter: Etymologisches Wörterbuch des deutschen Sprache*, 2nd ed. (Munich, 1988), pp. 374, 376. As for me, I remain persuaded that *Streifen* (stripe) and *strafen* (to punish) belong to the same family.

67. Which heraldry fully confirms, with the example of the Strasbourg coat of arms: *d'argent à la bande de gueules*; that is, a diagonal red stripe set on a white field. This is probably a matter of a graphic figure, creating word play between *Strasse* (taken here to mean "stripe") and *Strassburg*.

68. C. T. Onions, *The Oxford Dictionary of English Etymology* (Oxford, 1966), p. 876. Let us note here the link between "stripes" and the "striptease," both of which create scandal.

69. See A. Ernout and A. Meillet, *Dictionnaire étymologique de la langue latine*, 4th ed. (Paris, 1959), pp. 656–57.

70. Here we could contrast pajamas, a closed piece of clothing, with the chemise, an opened piece of clothing, and underline the "concentration camp" dimension of the first in relation to the second. Since they are striped, pajamas seem like a cage, which encloses the sleeper to better isolate him. Let us also note the link between the stripes on nightclothes and that in-between state that constitutes sleep; we find the same idea with pedestrian and railroad crossings, tents, etc. The stripe often has to do with intermediate places and states.

71. Here again, allow me to cite various studies I have published on the history of colors, especially the article listed in note 48 above, and those I've compiled in *Figures et couleurs: Etudes sur la symbolique et la sensibilité*

médiévales (Paris, 1986) and in *Couleurs, images, symboles: Etudes d'histoire et d'anthropologie* (Paris, 1989).

72. Nevertheless, there is not an equivalence between the white and the undyed. Until the seventeenth century, that is, until Newton's experiments and the discovery of the spectral organization of colors, white is considered a full-fledged color. While the undyed is, rather, to be found beside gray or grayish-brown or ecru. As for the colorless, it is completely different from white. In Western sensibility, the colorless is found beside the transparent or, as far as social codes are concerned, beside skin color. For matters of dress, this always constitutes "zero degree" for color; all articles of colored clothing are variations in relationship to it.

73. M. Kitchens, *When Underwear Counted, Being the Evolution of Underclothes* (Talladega, 1931); C. Willet and P. Cunnington, *The History of Underclothes* (London, 1951). Some information and ideas can be gleaned as well from P. Perrot, *Les Dessus and les dessous de la bourgeoisie* (Paris, 1981); and G. Vigarello, *Le Propre et le sale: L'hygiène du corps depuis le Moyen Age*, new ed. (Paris, 1985).

74. A long tradition—already evident in the feudal period—made cold colors the colors less *marked*, and thus less immodest, more pure, than warm colors. To dye material a cold color and make the coloring matter penetrate deeply into the fibers of the cloth remained for a long time more difficult an undertaking than to dye it a warm color. Which explains the faded appearance blue, green, and gray clothes had in all of Europe for many centuries. Now, between the faded and the pastel, there's no clear boundary, since, in both cases, it's a matter of diluted color.

75. I've borrowed this expression from Jean Baudrillard, *Le Système des objets* (Paris, 1968), p. 40.

76. The striped shirt even seems to have become a superlative form of the white shirt in contemporary French society, at least in the world of business. While executive management is often called "white collar" (as op-

posed to the workers who are "blue collar"), "super-management" henceforth tends to be labeled as "striped collar." See, for example, on the cover of *Le Point* magazine, no. 946 (November 26–December 2, 1990), the notice for an article entitled "Super-cadres: enquëte sur les cols rayés" [Super-executives: A report on the striped collars].

77. See note 58 above. Let us note that certain individuals suffering from stoutness deliberately wear horizontal stripes so that those who see them will attribute the visual impression of obesity to the stripes and not to the body. A subtle and perverse strategy of our age.

78. Despite abundant reading (the bibliography concerning sailor uniforms is prolific), I haven't found any information on the origin and expansion of seamen's striped clothing. Could the subject be taboo? Could the stripe, here again, be a sign of exclusion?

79. I thank my uncle, Henri Debief, for providing me with this bit of information and for drawing my attention to how the demeaning stripe has endured in the French navy.

80. W. Endreï, *L'Evolution des techniques du filage et du tissage, du Moyen Age à la révolution industrielle* (Paris, 1968); M. M. Grass, *History of Hosiery* (New York, 1955); A. Mortier, *Le Tricot et l'industrie de la bonneterie* (Troyes, 1891).

81. The stripes on ships' sails fulfill three functions: a technical function (to assemble pieces of cloth in order to form a large textile surface), an identifying function (a striped sail with two or many colors can be seen from a distance), and a dynamic function (inflated by the wind, a striped sail seems to move the ship forward more quickly than a plain sail; see note 57 above). That's why, today, in pleasure and competitive sailing, the spinnaker (the sail hoisted when the wind is from behind) is nearly always decorated with stripes.

82. E.M.C. Barraclough, *Yacht Flags and Ensigns* (London, 1951); O. Neubecker, *Fahnen und Flaggen* (Leipzig, 1939); W. Smith, *Flags through the Ages and across the World* (Maidenhead [Great Britain] 1975).

83. G. Jean-Aubry, *Eugène Boudin*, 2nd ed. (Paris, 1977); R. Schmit, *Eugène Boudin (1824–1898): Catalogue raisonné de l'oeuvre peint*, 3 vols. (Paris, 1973); J. Selz, *Eugène Boudin* (Paris, 1982).

84. G. Desert, *La Vie quotidienne sur les plages normandes du Second Empire aux années folles* (Paris, 1983); A. Hern, *The Seaside Holiday: The History of the English Seaside Resort* (London, 1967); J. Anderson and E. Swinglehurst, *The Victorian and Edwardian Seaside* (London, 1978); G. Renoy, *Bains de mer au temps des maillots rayés* (Brussels, 1976).

85. For the first half of the nineteenth century, see early remarks by J. Le-Coeur, *Des bains de mer: Guide médical et hygiénique du baigneur*, 2 vols. (Paris, 1846), which already recommends a two-color bathing suit.

86. See, above, the example of the banker and the gangster, who both wear striped suits.

87. D. Alexandre-Bidon, "Du drapeau à la cotte: vêtir l'enfant au Moyen Age (XIIIe–XVe s.)," *Cahiers du Léopard d'or*, vol. 1 (1989): 123–68.

88. Let us note in passing that the use of pink for little girls and sky blue for little boys, which appeared about the middle of the nineteenth century in France, England, and the United States, still awaits its ethnologists and historians. Not only does the appearance and widespread acceptance of this custom remain unknown, but its exact significance remains mysterious. None of the explanations proposed until now (notably religious ones) are very satisfying. For my part, it seems to me that it is, above all, a problem of social ethics (from which we get the use of pastel or unsaturated colors), but, even as a historian of colors, I confess to being unable to justify historically this distribution: pink for girls and blue for boys. Is it a matter of the declension of a feminine red and masculine black?

89. We must note that the only books available on the zebra in French are works for children. Like the pig, the dragon, and the fox, this animal is one of the rising stars in today's bestiary for infancy and childhood; whereas cats, dogs, rabbits, horses, and even bears are in clear decline.

90. The blouses of jockeys, a kind of "child" rider, merge the playful stripe, the emblematic stripe, the striped tied to chance and luck, and the stripe of children.

91. I must confess that even after dismantling, rather, dissecting (or is it "massacring"?) a tube of Signal® toothpaste, I don't understand how a bicolored paste striped like that can come out of a tube. For me, Signal® toothpaste retains all its mystery. It is probably better that way.

92. It goes without saying that the Signal® trademark has in no way "sponsored" my writing these few lines in praise of its toothpaste. Nevertheless, if, after the publication of this book, it would like to subsidize research on the history of stripes ...

93. M. Pastoureau, "Les couleurs du stade," *Vingtième Siècle: Revue d'histoire*, no. 26 (April–June 1990): 11–18.

94. On jockeys' blouses, see note 90 above.

95. I owe to my father, Henri Pastoureau, the juicy account of a visit he and Picasso made to a large clothing store, where the painter asked precisely for striped pants in order to, as he told the clerk, "stripe the ass." He even demanded that the stripes be vertical, which resulted in his leaving empty-handed.

96. Daniel Burren has often explained about his "interventions *in situ*," consisting of "putting [spaces and objects] into white and colored bands." For him, it is a matter of "punctuating," of "signaling without showing," of "giving volume to color," all functions the stripe has fulfilled for a very long time in Western culture. See D. Burren, *Entrevue: Conversation avec Anne Baldassari* (Paris, 1987). Very different from the works of Burren are the creations of Zebra, a group of German painters who, beginning in 1965, have chosen to break with abstraction and bring about "a return of the object in so far as any object is a prototype." The choice of the name, Zebra, doesn't carry with it the obligatory presence of stripes in the works of painters belonging to this group; it simply emphasizes the de-

sire to establish a distance from the painting in vogue, to "stripe them-selves," as Picasso would have said. See W. D. Dube, *The Zebra Group, 1965–1975: First Exhibition* (London, 1975).

97. Contemporary comic strips still present such figures—thieves or crooks—dressed in loud, horizontal stripes. In the Asterix adventure album, *La Serpe d'or*, for example, a horrid Gallo-roman *mafioso* wears a jersey with big yellow and black stripes.

98. In France, a newspaper like *Le Carnard enchainé* uses such an attribute excessively to depict dubious or disquieting political figures.

99. Moreover, this was probably already the case in the Middle Ages, at least if we are to believe the heraldic evidence, by which coats of arms formed from a *fascé* or a *palé d'argent et de gueules* are the ones most easily distinguished. But what about in other cultures? Has the recent extension of Western highway signs to the entire planet brought along with it visual acculturation phenomena as well?

100. H. Fillipetti and J. Trotereau, *Symboles et pratiques rituelles dans la maison paysanne traditionelle* (Paris, 1978). Sometimes, especially in Savoy, stripes take on the shape of chevrons, a superlative form that seems to offer even better protection.

101. This is the opinion of F. Truffaut (*Hitchcock* [Paris, 1984]); on the other hand, E. Rohmer and C. Chabrol (*Hitchcock* [Paris, 1975]) think that this is a "great film about love."

102. The film is an adaption of Francis Beeding's novel, *The House of the Dr. Edwards*. Hitchcock wanted to make it half in black and white, half in color, and film it entirely in an insane asylum, but the producer refused.

103. The jazz musicians' stripe is a dynamic one that brings together the stripes of the musician, the black man, and the traveling performer. The "jazzman" is located not only outside the social order but also outside the musical order (at least if we are considering the beginnings of jazz). He can't wear anything other than striped clothing.

104. Going still further, we can find this "putting in order" function again, which the stripe undeniably possesses, in the insignological use of striped ribbons for displaying decorations and proclaiming membership in an order of contemporary knighthood. The order stripe joins up here with the emblematic stripe.

105. Among aquarium fish (but not among butterflies), those displaying stripes are particularly sought after because they are rare. For collectors, their market value can be considerable.

106. Henceforth these bars are subject to competition by dots or patterns of dots, as the computer uses dots more than lines.

107. "To comb the giraffe" [a French expression for peforming some useless task], isn't this to put its spots in order, to try and make it into a zebra?

108. Is it going too far to see the wooden floor as a striped surface, and thus a dangerous surface, and thus to see the laying of a wall-to-wall carpet or a rug as a means of protecting oneself from it? Doesn't the floor made of strips of wood look like a trap? (But isn't the same thing true of striped rugs laid over it?)

109. By using stripes, the print finds a means for making certain areas of an image more dense or darkening them. Thus, thanks to the stripe, the black and white image often merges the parameters of luminosity and saturation.

110. D. K. Bennett, "Stripes Do Not a Zebra Make," in *Systematic Zoology*, vol. 29 (1980): 272–87; S. J. Gould, "A propos de zébrures," in *Quand les poules auront des dents* (Paris, 1984), pp. 391–403.

111. Many manuals for painters explain the effects of illusion the artist can obtain by beginning with a striped surface. Many propose the visual exercises that are found in all works on optics. Throughout, the stripe is presented as a trompe-l'oeil. Among all these works, the most pertinent seem to me to be those developed by the Bauhaus theoreticians.

112. From which we get the use of the stripe in the art of camouflage. Since

World War I, for example, it isn't unusual to paint the hull and deck of certain warships with motifs in the form of stripes ("dazzled patterns") meant to fool submarine periscopes. See N. Wilkinson, *The Dazzle Painting of Ships* (Newcastle, 1919) and the catalog from the show *Camouflage*, held at the Imperial War Museum of London in March–April 1989 (I thank Henry Colomer for providing me with these references). As far as animals are concerned, zoologists have concluded that the tiger's stripes allow it to pass unnoticed in its natural habitat and to better watch for prey, whereas those of the zebra deceive no predator and thus do not protect it at all. On the other hand, they help the zebra to recognize its fellow creatures immediately and, in the case of danger, facilitate a herd flight, more effective for the survival of the species. See the studies cited in note 110 above.

Index

masculine stripes, 68–69, 81

Maupassant, Guy de, 81

Memling, Hans, 22

mendicant orders, 8, 10, 102–3(n7)

mercenaries, 41

military stripes, 41, 53, 79

Millaud, Pierre de, 11

millers, 17

minstrels, 76, 86, 87

mi-parti dress, 37–38, 43

Montagnard Convention, 50

moral axis, x–xi

mural paintings, 16

musica, 88

musical stripes, 81, 83, 86–88, 90, 118(n103)

Muslims, 12, 14, 90, 104(n17)

mystery felines, 107(n32)

Nestor (comic strip butler), 40

Nicholas, Saint, 15

nightclothes, 63

non-Christians, 14, 17

Obélix (comic strip character), 76

obstacle stripes, 58, 61, 67, 113(n70)

Oceania Indians, 40

onager, 24, 106(n29)

order, 4, 88, 90, 119(n104)

Oriental fabric, 11–12

outcasts, 2, 16–17, 61, 75, 90; musicians, 86–88

paintings, 16, 20, 22, 39–40

pajamas, 61, 63, 113(n70)

parti, 17, 105(n20)

partitions, 27

pastels, 65–67, 75, 116(n88)

Pastoreau, Henri, 117(n95)

patterned surfaces, 19, 20–21

peasant stripe, 48

pedestrian crossings, 85

penal colonies, 56, 110(n51)

Picasso, Pablo, 81, 82, 117(n95), 118(n96)

Pieds nickelés, 83

Plague, 42

plain surfaces, 19, 20, 25

planes, 25–28

playful stripes, 76–78, 117(n90)

plow, 90

political stripes, 46

positivism, 12

poverty, 102(n7)

prisoners' stripes, 4, 16, 55–61, 81

prostitutes, 13–14, 15, 17, 25

protective stripes, 61, 67, 85–86

European Perspectives

A Series in Social Thought and Cultural Criticism

LAWRENCE D. KRITZMAN, EDITOR